ESL Conversation Rocket

A Scaffolded, Grammar-Based
Conversation Workbook for
ESL Learners

— Brian Branca —

ESL Conversation Rocket

A Scaffolded, Grammar-Based Conversation Workbook for ESL Learners

Copyright © 2019 by ESL Publishing

All rights reserved. This book or any portion thereof may not be reproduced or used in any manner whatsoever without the express written permission of the publisher, except for the use of brief quotations in a book review.

ISBN: 978-0-9986965-6-0

Printed in the United States of America
First Printing, 2019

Cover art by Daniel Branca

ESL Publishing
WWW.ESLPUBLISHING.COM

ESL Publishing is dedicated to producing quality books for English language learners.

A NOTE FOR TEACHERS

Please **do not** photocopy this book. We are a small publishing company. Please visit our website *www.eslpublishing.com* for specials and bulk discounts.

Thank you!

Table of Contents

Acknowledgments v
What is Scaffolded, Grammar-Based Conversation? vii
How to Use This Book ix
Introduction: What is Conversation? 1

Part 1

Unit 1: What Chores Do You Do? 4
Unit 2: What Did You Do Last Weekend? 15
Unit 3: How Often Do You Eat Pizza? 28
Unit 4: What Are You Going To Do After Class? 38
Everyday Language Review Part 1 49
Reaction Response Part 1 52
Be the Teacher Part 1 54
Conversation Test Part 1 56

Part 2

Unit 5: Because and So 63
Unit 6: Which Is More Delicious, Pizza or Broccoli? 71
Unit 7: What Animal Is The Cutest? 82
Unit 8: Which Do You Prefer, Soccer or Basketball? 92
Unit 9: What Country Should I Visit? 101
Unit 10: If It Rains, What Will You Do? 112
Everyday Language Review Part 2 122
Reaction Response Part 2 127
Be the Teacher Part 2 129
Conversation Test Part 2 131

About the Author 139

See other titles by ESL Publishing at the end of the book!

Acknowledgments

To YEJ and HGB:

I lovingly dedicate this book to you.

Thank you to my creative and talented brother, Daniel Branca. Not only did he create the cover for this book but he is also my partner at www.myenglisheets.com. Daniel's work has helped teachers and students around the globe access free, high-quality ESL/EFL materials. You can contact him at: www.danielbranca.com and designerdanb@gmail.com. You're the best, Daniel. The best.

To all of my students, from the West Side of Chicago to the south side of Korea: I have done my best to teach you English and you have taught me one very important life lesson: underneath superficial differences like language and skin color, we are all the same. The experiences I have shared with you inspired me to write this book.

To Jeane Slone of ESL Publishing: Thank you for giving me this opportunity and thank you for your supportive guidance throughout the publishing process.

To Sandy Davenport, ESL teacher at Pittsburg Adult Education Center in Pittsburg, CA: Thank you for your ideas and constructive criticism. Your insights gave me a virtual foot inside the American ESL classroom, which helped drastically improve the final draft of this book.

To Cris Wanzer of Manuscripts to Go: Thank you for your patience and hard work. This is my rookie effort, so I am grateful for your understanding and diligence. www.ManuscriptsToGo.com

What is Scaffolded, Grammar-Based Conversation?

After spending several years teaching English language learners of all levels, I've come to realize that there are few books that effectively teach English conversation. Further, I've found that many of the "speaking" and "conversation" books out there are, by and large, inaccessible for beginner and low-level language learners. This realization is what inspired me to write this book. The object is to get beginner and low-level students speaking with confidence and competence.

The problem with many English language conversation books is that there is no scaffolding. Imagine teaching a child to ride a bike without training wheels; the experience would be frustrating and painful. Herein lies the key to effective English conversation instruction. English conversation should be taught via scaffolding so students feel comfortable and confident from the outset. Scaffolding is creating a bridge from what students already know (skills and life experiences) to the new skill or competency to be acquired (in this case, conversations in English). The key to good scaffolding is using students' prior knowledge as a starting point to build a new skill. Each unit of this book uses a simple and easily accessible grammar skill as that starting point. From there, students utilize this understanding to gradually build competence in "real-life conversation." In each unit, students practice with six exercises which gradually build in difficulty. Each unit culminates in "Real-Life Conversation," where students have a chance to practice speaking with a partner.

In my experience, the English language resource market is full of two kinds of books: 1) Mostly grammar without any real, authentic conversation; or 2) All conversation and no scaffolding. ESL Conversation Rocket is a hybrid of the two. The result is a student-centered book in which students use their understanding of simple grammar points, as well as their personal life experiences, to have real, authentic conversations in English. The conversation practice helps students see how people naturally interact in various situations, and the grammar helps students make the interaction successful.

ESL Conversation Rocket is written specifically for beginners and low-level learners, so the teacher may have to introduce some new terms but not many because a very limited vocabulary is used and recycled throughout the book. This allows students to really focus on framing their responses without getting sidetracked by lots of new words.

How to Use This Book

Each unit follows the same basic format:

Introduction
The introduction includes a basic grammar lesson. All of the activities in each unit are based on the grammar point in the introduction. It serves as the foundation for each unit.

Preparation 1
This exercise is designed to be completely individual (as opposed to with a partner). Here the students are doing a simple practice of what they learned in the introduction.

Preparations 2-3
These are structured, partner-speaking activities. As such, students should not be able to see their partner's information. Each activity should be modeled by the teacher before the students begin working.

Practice
This is another individual activity and a great homework assignment. Here, students are creating a grammatically correct script for the last section in the unit (Real-Life Conversation). This section should be checked so that any grammar-related misunderstandings are corrected before the student begins a conversation.

Model Conversations
Here the students are looking at examples of conversation. The model conversations include Reaction Responses and Tell-Me-More Questions. In the second conversation, the students are to fill in the blanks with the appropriate Reaction Responses and Tell-Me-More Questions.

Text Me
Another partner activity. The partners should send "text messages" without talking by passing their books back and forth. This is a silent writing activity.

Real-Life Conversation
This is a pure speaking activity. Partners interview each other with the questions provided. Students should attempt to use Reaction Responses, Tell-Me-More Questions, and Everyday Language in the conversation.

Everyday Language Tips
These language tips serve to enhance student understanding of how native English speakers use idioms and colloquialisms in everyday conversation.

Reaction Responses and Tell-Me-More Questions Practice
This gives students some more targeted practice with Reaction Responses and Tell-Me-More Questions before the speaking test.

Be the Teacher
Here, the students evaluate sample conversations. The objective is for the students to understand how they will be evaluated by applying a rubric to sample student conversations. They get to grade conversations just like a teacher would.

Conversation Tests
Students first choose their own test questions and then have a conversation with their partner.

Grade Your Test
If students opted to record their conversation test, they would then go back and evaluate themselves just like in "Be the Teacher."

Rubrics
The rubrics are the backbone of the book. Students should be familiar with the rubrics before they have their first conversation. In addition, the rubrics should be used to evaluate all conversation throughout the book. The rubrics are purposely simple and student-friendly so that they can be used by teachers to evaluate students **OR** by students themselves for self-assessment/partner-assessment.

Notebook
Have students keep a notebook to compile a list of Reaction Responses, Tell-Me-More Questions, and Everyday Language Tips. Also, encourage students to add their own personal examples (from TV, movies, outside-of-class conversation, etc.) to the notebook.

Part 1

Introduction: What is Conversation?

Look at the two examples. Which is an example of conversation?

Example 1	Example 2
A: What's your favorite food? B: Pizza.	A: What's your favorite food? B: Pizza. How about you? A: That's a hard question. I love so many foods. I think chicken is my favorite food. B: Oh yeah? What kind of chicken do you like? B: I like spicy fried chicken. A: That sounds delicious. Now I'm hungry!

If you said Example 2, you are correct. In Example 1, there is only a question and an answer. Conversation is more than just a question and an answer. Conversation should include **Reaction Responses** and **Tell-Me-More Questions**. **Reaction Responses** and **Tell-Me-More Questions** make conversations longer and more interesting.

Questions + Answers + Reaction Responses + Tell-Me-More Questions
= Great Conversation

What are **Reaction Responses**?
Reaction Responses show interest, surprise, confusion, empathy, or another feeling or emotion toward something your conversation partner says.
Examples **Reaction Responses** that show **interest**: - That's cool. - Got it. - Is that right? **Reaction Responses** that show **empathy**: - That's too bad. - I'm sorry to hear that. **Reaction Responses** that show **surprise**: - For real? - Wow! - No way!

What are Tell-Me-More Questions?
Tell-Me-More Questions are follow-up questions (they come *after* the initial question/statement) which ask the conversation partner to give more information.
Tell-More-Questions usually begin with: what, why, how, when, where. - **What** kind of pizza do you like? - **Why** do you like pizza? - **How** often do you eat pizza? - **When** do you usually eat pizza? - **Where** do you buy your pizza?

Look at the conversation again and notice the **Reaction Responses** and Tell-Me-More Questions.

A: What's your favorite food?
B: Pizza. How about you?
A: **That's a hard question**. I love so many foods. I think chicken is my favorite food.
B: **Oh yeah?** What kind of chicken do you like?
B: I like spicy fried chicken.
A: **That sounds delicious. Now I'm hungry!**

Your Turn

Directions: read the conversation. Underline the **Reaction Responses** and circle the **Tell-Me-More Questions**.

A: What time do you wake up in the morning?

B: I usually wake up at 5:30 a.m.

A: Wow! That's super early! Why do you wake up so early?

B: I like to exercise, shower, and eat a big breakfast. You?

A: I wake at 9 a.m. I like to sleep!

B: That's cool.

Now, think about your own daily conversations. Can you think of the **Reaction Responses** and **Tell-Me-More Questions** that you use? Write them in the empty spaces below.

Reaction Responses	Tell-Me-More Questions
1. That's a hard question.	1. **How** about you?
2. Oh yeah?	2. **What kind** of chicken do you like?
3. That sounds delicious. Now I'm hungry!	3. **Why** do you wake up so early?
4. Wow!	4. You? (=How about you?)
5. That's super early!	Your own
6. That's cool.	
Your own	_____
	_____
_____	_____
_____	
_____	

Put it Together
So, what is conversation?

_____

_____

1. What Chores Do You Do?

Introduction

The **simple present tense** describes:

1) **Routines and Habits**
   - ✓ He <u>works</u> at a factory.
   - ✓ I <u>exercise</u> in the gym.

2) **Facts**
   - ✓ I <u>go</u> to high school.
   - ✓ Los Angeles <u>is</u> a big city.

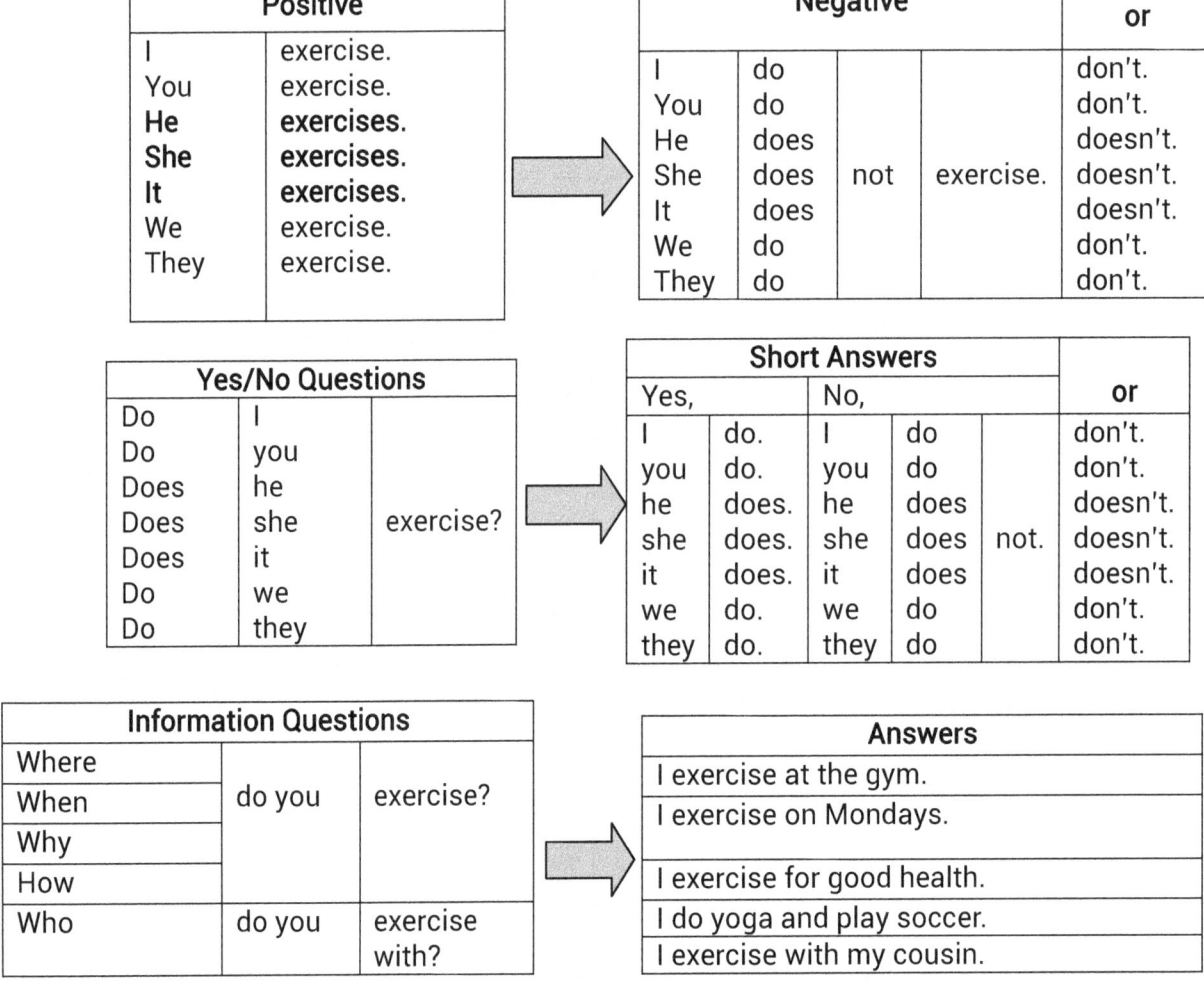

Positive	
I	exercise.
You	exercise.
He	**exercises.**
She	**exercises.**
It	**exercises.**
We	exercise.
They	exercise.

Negative				or
I	do			don't.
You	do			don't.
He	does			doesn't.
She	does	not	exercise.	doesn't.
It	does			doesn't.
We	do			don't.
They	do			don't.

Yes/No Questions		
Do	I	
Do	you	
Does	he	
Does	she	exercise?
Does	it	
Do	we	
Do	they	

Short Answers					or
Yes,		No,			
I	do.	I	do		don't.
you	do.	you	do		don't.
he	does.	he	does		doesn't.
she	does.	she	does	not.	doesn't.
it	does.	it	does		doesn't.
we	do.	we	do		don't.
they	do.	they	do		don't.

Information Questions		
Where		
When	do you	exercise?
Why		
How		
Who	do you	exercise with?

Answers
I exercise at the gym.
I exercise on Mondays.
I exercise for good health.
I do yoga and play soccer.
I exercise with my cousin.

Unit 1: Key Question and Answer
Q: What chores do you do?
A: I **vacuum** the living room and **wash** the dishes.

Preparation I

Directions: Read, listen, and fill-in the blanks with your partner. Student A reads first and Partner B fills in the blanks on the next page.

Student A

You read, Student B writes

Ravi's Day

Ravi **gets** up at 6:30 a.m. Next, he goes to the kitchen and **has** breakfast. Ravi also **feeds** his puppy, Rocco. Ravi and Rocco **love** breakfast. After eating, Ravi **takes** a shower, brushes his teeth, and **gets** dressed. He then **rides** his bike to school. Ravi's favorite subjects are **history** and **science.**

Student B reads, you write

After school, Ravi _____ his homework and _____ a snack. He then _____ his friends at the park and _____ baseball or soccer. Ravi _____ home at 6:30 for _____. When dinner is finished, he _____ with his puppy and _____ TV. Ravi then _____ his face and _____ his teeth. He _____ to bed at 10 p.m.

Preparation I

Directions: Read, listen, and fill-in the blanks with your partner. Student A reads first and you fill in the blanks.

Student B

Student A reads, you write

Ravi's Day

Ravi _____ up at 6:30 a.m. Next, he goes to the kitchen and _____ breakfast. Ravi also _____ his puppy, Rocco. Ravi and Rocco _____ breakfast. After eating, Ravi _____ a shower, brushes his teeth, and _____ dressed. He then _____ his bike to school. Ravi's favorite subjects are _____ and _____.

You read, Student A writes

After school, Ravi **does** his homework and **eats** a snack. He then **meets** his friends at the park and **plays** baseball or soccer. Ravi **runs** home at 6:30 for **dinner**. When dinner is finished, he **plays** with his puppy and **watches** TV. Ravi then **washes** his face and **brushes** his teeth. He **goes** to bed at 10 p.m.

Preparation II

Directions: Complete the info-gap activity with your partner. **Partner B goes first** and asks a question about an empty square. Then, **Partner A** asks a question.

Target Language

Partner B: How does Max relax?

Partner A: Max **reads books** to relax.

A

	How does ___ relax?	What does ___ do in his/her free time?	What does ___ do after school?	What does ___ do on the weekends?	What chore does ___ do?
Max	reads books		plays drums		does laundry
Hana		plays soccer		goes to church	
Ravi	does puzzles		eats a snack		vacuums
Sally		exercises		sleeps late	
You					

Ask your partner:
How do **you** relax?
What do **you** do _____?
What chores do **you** do?

Preparation II

Directions: Complete the info-gap activity with your partner. **Partner B goes first** and asks a question about an empty square. Then, **Partner A** asks a question.

Target Language

Partner B: How does Max relax?

Partner A: Max **reads books** to relax.

B

	How does ___ relax?	What does ___ do in his/her free time?	What does ___ do after school?	What does ___ do on the weekends?	What chore does ___ do?
Max		listens to music		goes to the movies	
Hana	does yoga		studies Chinese		washes dishes
Ravi		plays with friends		goes hiking	
Sally	draws pictures		goes to the library		takes the garbage out
You					

Ask your partner:
How do **you** relax?
What do **you** do _____?
What chores do **you** do?

Preparation III

Directions: Write 10 sentences (or more!) about your daily routine. Use the activities below to help you.

go to school	wash my face	do homework	brush my teeth
eat a snack	exercise	watch TV	hang out with friends
eat (breakfast, lunch, dinner)	get up	go to bed	argue with my brother/sister husband/wife
clean my room	go home	play smartphone games	play outside
wash the dishes	walk the dog	take the garbage out	do the laundry
go to work	come home from work	pick up children from school	cook dinner

I get up at_____

_____

_____

_____

_____

_____

_____

_____

Everyday Language Tip

hit the books = to study very hard

Ex.
I'm sorry, I can't go to the movies tonight. I have to **hit the books** because I have a test tomorrow.

Practice

Directions: Answer the questions with 1 or 2 sentences. Use the **present tense.**

Example: What time do you go to bed?
I go to bed at 10:30 p.m. on weekdays. I go to bed at 11:30 on weekends.

① What TV shows do you watch?
_____

② What do you do in your free time?
_____

③ What time do you wake up in the morning?
_____

④ What are two of your hobbies?
_____

⑤ What chores do you do at home?
_____

⑥ What do you do on the weekends?
_____

⑦ What music do you like to listen to?
_____

⑧ What desserts do you like?
_____

⑨ When do you go to bed at night?
_____

⑩ What exercise do you like to do?
_____

Now, write your own present-tense question and answer it.

Question:_____?

Answer: _____.

Everyday Language Tip

couch potato = a lazy person

Ex.
During the week I am so busy with school and work. On the weekends, I like to be a **couch potato**.

Model Conversations

Directions: Read the conversations with your partner. Pay attention to the **Reaction Responses** and **Tell-Me-More Questions**. Add these responses and questions to your notebook.

Reaction Responses (rr) are used to respond or react.	Tell-Me-More Questions (tmmq) ask for more information.
• That's cool. • I see. • _____ • _____ • _____	• How about you? • When...? • Do you...? • _____ • _____

A: What do you like to do?

B: I like to go hiking. **How about you?** *(tmmq)*

A: I love to play soccer.

B: **I see.** *(rr)* **When do you go hiking?** *(tmmq)*

A: I go hiking every Sunday morning. **Do you have other hobbies?** *(tmmq)*

B: I love cooking. My best recipe is spaghetti.

A: **That's cool.** *(rr)*

Tip
In your notebook, keep a list of all the RRs, TMMQs and Everyday Language.

Directions: Now, fill in the blanks with the **Reaction Responses** and **Tell-Me-More Questions** from the conversation.

I see.   When...?   That's cool   How about you?

A: What TV shows do you watch?

B: My favorite TV show is "Infinite Challenge." _____?

A: I don't really like any TV shows. I just watch the news.

B: _____. _____do you watch the news?

A: I watch the news in the evening. Do you watch other TV shows?

B: Yes, I also like to watch soccer on Saturday morning.

A: _____.

Text Me

Directions: Create a text conversation with your partner by passing your book back and forth. Make sure to include Reaction Responses and Tell-Me-More Questions! *No talking!*

A: What do you do in your free time?

B: I_____. You?

A:

B:

A:

B:

A:

B:

Grade Yourself!		
Level 1	Level 2	Level 3
Conversation Amateur	Conversation Rookie	Conversation Pro
▲ Asks or answers a question	▲ Asks or answers a question ■ Uses a Reaction Response	▲ Asks or answers a question ■ Uses a Reaction Response ★ Asks a Tell-Me-More Question

Real-Life Conversation

Directions: For each question, have a short conversation with Student B. Try to use the **Reaction Responses and Tell-Me-More Questions** in your conversation.

Student A

- What TV shows do you watch?
- What do you do in your free time?
- What time do you wake up in the morning?
- What are two of your hobbies?
- What chores do you do at home?
- What do you do before English class?
- What do you drink in the morning?
- What do you do before school or work?
- What do you do before bed?
- What activities do you do with your friends?

Conversation Checklist

- I <u>asked</u> a question.
- I <u>answered</u> a question.
- I used a **Reaction Response**.
- I asked a **Tell-Me-More-Question**.

Real-Life Conversation

Directions: For each question, have a short conversation with Student A. Try to use the **Reaction Responses and Tell-Me-More Questions** in your conversation.

Student B

- What do you do on the weekends?
- What music do you like to listen to?
- What desserts do you like?
- When do you go to bed at night?
- What exercise do you like to do?
- How do you relax after school or work?
- What kind of foreign food do you like?
- What kind of books do you like to read?
- What do you do after English class?
- What smartphone apps do you use?

Conversation Checklist

- ○ I asked a question.
- ○ I answered a question.
- ○ I used a **Reaction Response**.
- ○ I asked a **Tell-Me-More-Question**.

2. What Did You Do Last Weekend?

Introduction

The **past tense** indicates that an action has finished.

Examples
- I <u>ate</u> chicken last night.
- We <u>visited</u> Paris last summer vacation.
- I <u>went</u> to university for four years.

Positive		Negative				or
I	exercised.	I	did			
You	exercised.	You	did			
He	exercised.	He	did			
She	exercised.	She	did	not	exercise.	didn't.
It	exercised.	It	did			
We	exercised.	We	did			
They	exercised.	They	did			

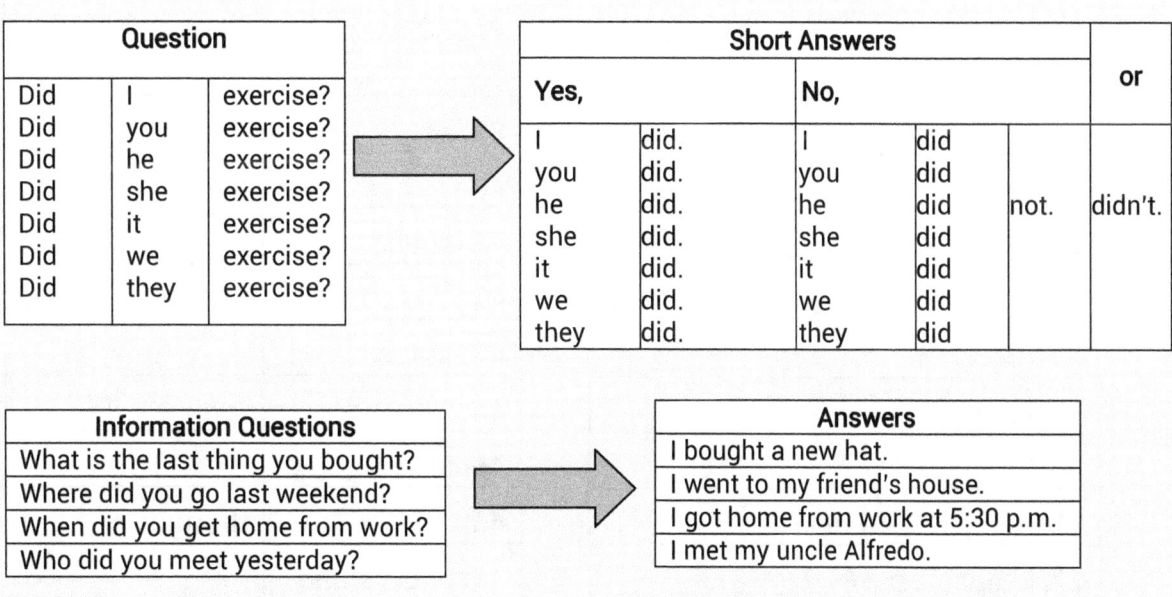

Information Questions
What is the last thing you bought?
Where did you go last weekend?
When did you get home from work?
Who did you meet yesterday?

Answers
I bought a new hat.
I went to my friend's house.
I got home from work at 5:30 p.m.
I met my uncle Alfredo.

Unit 2: Key Question and Answer
Q: What <u>did</u> you do last weekend?
A: I <u>bought</u> a new jacket last weekend.

Irregular Verb Practice

Directions: write the correct verb form in the empty space.

Present Tense	Past Tense
1. become	
2.	began
3. buy	
4.	broke
5. bring	
6.	built
7. choose	
8.	came
9. cut	
10. draw	
11.	drove
12.	fell
13. feel	
14. find	
15. get	
16.	gave
17.	went
18. grow	
19. hear	
20. hit	
21.	held
22. keep	
23. know	
24.	led
25.	left

Present Tense	Past Tense
26.	let
27. lie	
28. lose	
29.	made
30. meet	
31.	paid
32. put	
33. read	
34.	rose
35. run	
36.	said
37. see	
38.	sent
39. set	
40.	sat
41. spend	
42.	spoke
43. stand	
44.	took
45. tell	
46.	thought
47. understand	
48. wake	
49.	wore
50. write	

Preparation I

Directions: For 1-5, change the verb to the past tense.

Part 1
Example

(give) I _gave_ my sister a book for her birthday.

1. (make) Teresa _____ delicious tacos last night.

2. (go) I _____ to bed at 11:30.

3. (eat / is) I _____ beans and rice for dinner. It _____ very delicious.

4. (build) Michaela _____ a sandcastle at the beach last weekend.

5. (see) I _____ Spiderman last month at the movie theater.

Part 2

Directions: Use the list of irregular verbs to complete each sentence.

6. Juan _____ a letter to his sick grandmother.

7. I _____ a picture in art class yesterday.

8. My mother _____ me a new smartphone yesterday!

9. My son likes to exercise. Last night, he _____ in the park.

10. I finished work at 5:30. I _____ home at 6:00 pm.

11. Haru _____ the door for her father.

Everyday Language Tip

have a blast = have a great time

Ex.
Last weekend we went to a baseball game. We **had a blast!**

Preparation II

Body Language Crossword

Directions: Take turns using body language to act out each past-tense verb. No talking or making sounds. (Laughing is OK! ☺)

Student A

Useful Sentences
- ✓ Look at #___ across.
- ✓ Look at #___ down.
- ✓ More body language please!

No Peeking!

Put a blank piece of paper between these pages so you can't see your partner's information!

Preparation II

Body Language Crossword

Directions: Use body language to act out each past-tense verb. No talking or making sounds. (Laughing is OK! ☺)

Student B

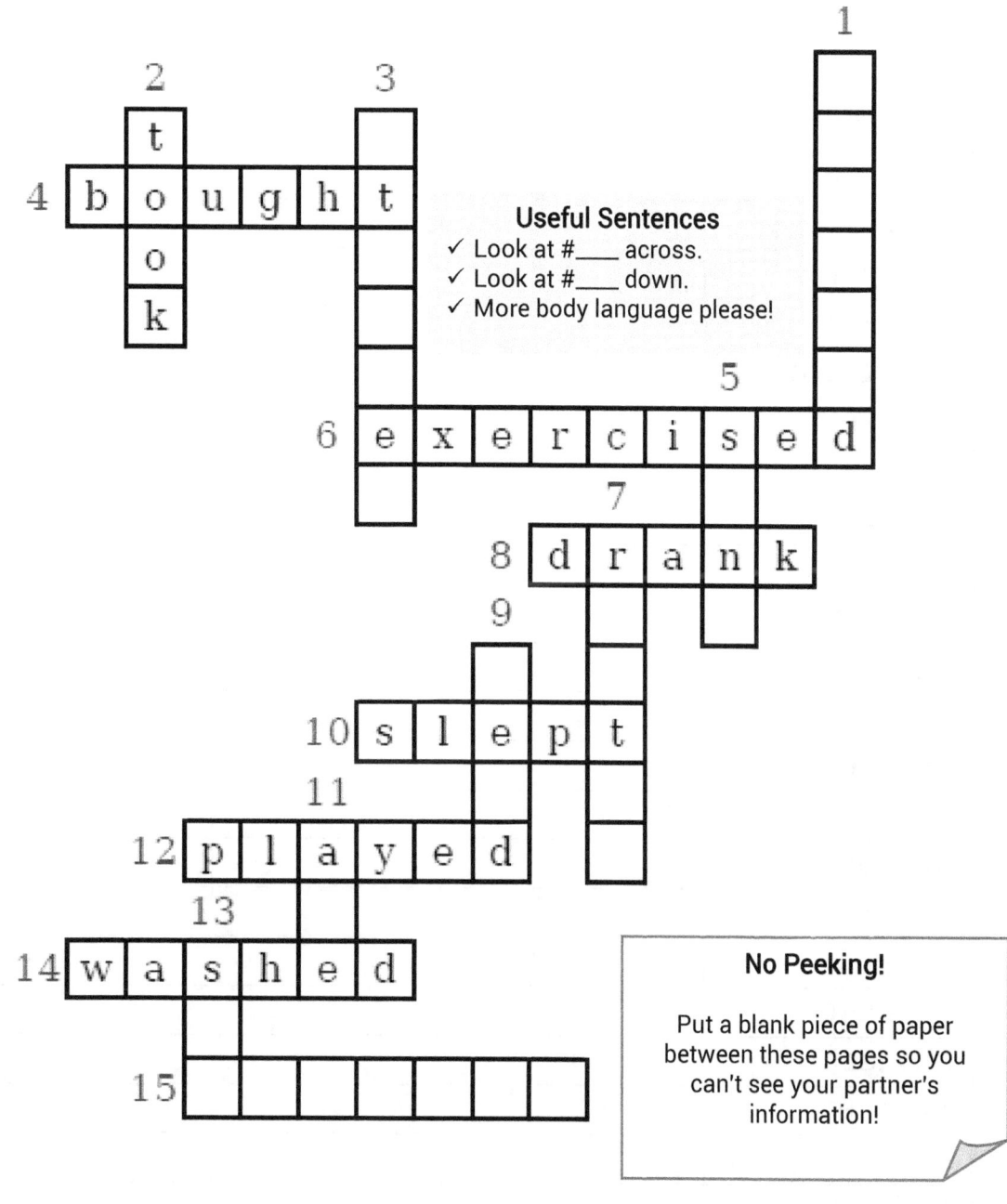

Useful Sentences
- ✓ Look at #___ across.
- ✓ Look at #___ down.
- ✓ More body language please!

No Peeking!

Put a blank piece of paper between these pages so you can't see your partner's information!

Preparation III

Past-Tense Quiz

> **No Peeking!**
> Put a blank piece of paper between these pages so you can't see page 21!

Directions: Write the regular and irregular verbs in the past tense. Be careful of spelling!

Present Tense	Past Tense	Correct	Incorrect
1. wake			
2. drink			
3. wash			
4. is			
5. rest			
6. do			
7. lose			
8. listen			
9. brush			
10. prepare			
11. take			
12. play			
13. buy			
14. sweep			
15. watch			
16. go			
17. send			
18. boil			
19. sleep			
20. read			
21. fry			
22. are			
23. search			
24. clean			
25. meet			
26. arrive			
27. have			
	Total		

Preparation IV

Directions: Complete the info-gap activity with your partner. Student A reads first.

My Busy Weekend
Student A

You read, Student B writes

On Saturday morning, I **slept** late. At 10:30 a.m., I **did** my chores. I **swept** the floor, **cleaned** my room, and **took** the garbage out. After doing chores, I **watched** a soccer game on TV. I love soccer, but my favorite team lost. I **was** pretty upset. In the afternoon, I **met** my friends at the park. We **played** badminton, **sent** funny text messages, and **listened** to music on our smartphones. After meeting my friends, my mom and I took the bus to the department store. We **bought** a warm sweater for my dad's birthday. We **arrived** home at 6:30 p.m. and **prepared** dinner. After dinner, I **read** my favorite comic book, **brushed** my teeth, and **went** to bed at 10:00 p.m.

You write, Student B reads

On Sunday morning, I _____ and searched for delicious breakfast recipes on the internet. Next, I fried bacon and _____ some eggs for my dad's birthday breakfast. He was so happy! After breakfast, we _____. We rested at the lake and _____ pictures. After one hour, we were tired and hungry, so we took a break at the local coffee shop. Mom and Dad _____ and I had chocolate milk and a doughnut. In the afternoon, I _____. Later in the evening, I watched my favorite TV show. After dinner, I _____, washed my face, and _____. It was a busy weekend!

Preparation IV

Directions: Complete the info-gap activity with your partner. Student A reads first.

My Busy Weekend
Student B

You write, Student A reads

On Saturday morning, I _____. At 10:30 a.m., I did my chores. I cleaned my room, swept the floor and _____. After doing chores, I _____ on TV. I love soccer, but my favorite team lost. I was pretty upset. In the afternoon, I _____. We played badminton, _____, and listened to music on our smartphones. After meeting my friends, my mom and I took the bus to the department store. We _____ for my dad's birthday. We arrived home at 6:30 p.m. and prepared dinner. After dinner, I _____, brushed my teeth and _____.

You read, Student A writes

On Sunday morning, I **woke** up early and **searched** for delicious breakfast recipes on the internet. Next, I **fried** bacon and **boiled** some eggs for my dad's birthday breakfast. He **was** so happy! After breakfast, we **went** for a long bike ride. We **rested** at the lake and **took** beautiful nature pictures. After one hour, we **were** tired and hungry, so we **took** a break at the local coffee shop. Mom and Dad **drank** hot coffee and I **had** chocolate milk and a doughnut. In the afternoon, I **took** a nap. Later in the evening, I **watched** my favorite TV show. After dinner, I **did** my math homework, **washed** my face, and **went** to bed early. It was a busy weekend!

Practice

Directions: Answer the questions with 1-2 sentences. Use the past tense.

Example
What did you do last weekend?
Last weekend I **went** to the movies. I saw an action movie.

① What time did you go to sleep last night?
_____

② What TV show did you watch last weekend?
_____

③ What was the last board game you played?
_____

④ Who did you send a text message to yesterday?
_____

⑤ What is the last thing you bought?
_____

⑥ What did you do this morning?
_____

⑦ What did you drink with breakfast?
_____

⑧ What did you do for your last birthday?
_____

⑨ Where did you go on your last school trip?
_____

Now, write your own past tense question and answer it.

Question:_____?

Answer: _____

Everyday Language Tip

call it a day = to finish work

Ex.
After studying for two hours, we **called it a day**. We were very tired.

Model Conversations

Directions: Read the conversations with your partner. Pay attention to the **Reaction Responses** and **Tell-Me-More Questions**. Add these responses and questions to your notebook.

A **Reaction Response (rr)** is used to respond or react.	**Tell-Me-More Questions (tmmq)** ask for more information.
Oh yeah? Sounds _____. (good, fun, interesting, relaxing, etc) _____ _____ _____	How about you? / You? What did you…? Where did you…? _____ _____ _____

A: Did you go to the park yesterday?

B: Yes, I did.

A: **What did you do there? (tmmq)**

B: I sat on a bench and read a book. **What did you do? (tmmq)**

A: **Sounds relaxing! (rr)** I just watched a movie. It was boring.

B: **Oh yeah? (rr) Where did you watch the movie? (tmmq)**

A: I watched the movie at home.

B: **Sounds cool! (rr)**

Directions: Now, fill in the blanks with the **Reaction Responses** and **Tell-Me-More Questions**.

What did you…? (2x) Oh yeah? Where did you…? Sounds _____!

A: What did you do last weekend?

B: I went to the zoo with my family.

A: _____? _____ see at the zoo?

B: I saw monkeys, elephants, and a parrot. _____! _____ do last weekend?

A: I visited my grandparents last weekend.

B: _____ go with your grandparents?

A: We went for a walk at the beach and then ate dinner at a seafood restaurant.

Text Me

Directions: Create a text conversation with your partner by passing your book back and forth. *No talking!*

A: What did you do last weekend?

B: _____. What about you?

A:

B:

A:

B:

A:

B:

Grade Yourself!		
Level 1	**Level 2**	**Level 3**
Conversation Amateur	Conversation Rookie	Conversation Pro
▲ Asks or answers a question	▲ Asks or answers a question ■ Uses a Reaction Response	▲ Asks or answers a question ■ Uses a Reaction Response ★ Asks a Tell-Me-More Question

Real-Life Conversation

Directions: For each question, have a short conversation with Student B. Try to use **Reaction Responses** and **Tell-Me-More Questions** in your conversation.

Student A

- What time did you go to sleep last night?
- What TV show did you watch last weekend?
- What was the last board game you played?
- Who turned out the lights?
- What is the last thing you bought?
- What homework did you do last night?
- What chore did you do last week?
- What was your favorite toy as a child?
- Where did you live when you were five years old?

Conversation Checklist

- ◯ I asked a question.
- ◯ I answered a question.
- ◯ I used a **Reaction Response**.
- ◯ I asked a **Tell-Me-More-Question**.

Real-Life Conversation

Directions: For each question, have a short conversation with Student A. Try to use **Reaction Responses** and **Tell-Me-More Questions** in your conversation.

Student B
- What did you do this morning?
- What did you drink with breakfast?
- What did you do for your last birthday?
- Where did you go on your last school trip?
- What was the last salty snack you ate?
- What did you do on Sunday afternoon?
- What did you eat for dinner last night?
- What was the last wild animal you saw?
- What was the last fruit you ate?
- What was the last sweet snack you ate?

Conversation Checklist

- ○ I <u>asked</u> a question.
- ○ I <u>answered</u> a question.
- ○ I used a **Reaction Response**.
- ○ I asked a **Tell-Me-More-Question**.

3. How Often Do You Eat Pizza?

Introduction

We can use **adverbs of indefinite or definite frequency** to answer **"How often...?"** questions.

		adverbs	example sentence
indefinite frequency	More often --→ ←----- Less often	always	I always eat pizza.
		usually	I usually eat pizza.
		often	I often eat pizza.
		sometimes	I sometimes eat pizza.
		occasionally	I occasionally eat pizza.
		seldom	I seldom eat pizza.
		rarely	I rarely eat pizza.
		almost never	I almost never eat pizza.
		never	I never eat pizza.

indefinite frequency adverb rules

subject + adverb + verb (non "be" verb)
I <u>never</u> eat pizza.

subject + "be" verb + adverb
My puppy is <u>almost always</u> hungry.

	Be more specific!	
definite frequency	once twice several times one hundred times	a second/ a minute/ an hour / a day / a week / every two weeks/ a month / a year
	every	second / minute / hour / day / week / other week / month / year / five years/ ten years
	Definite frequency adverbs can come at the beginning or end of the sentence. *Notice the comma!* I eat pizza **<u>every two weeks.</u>** **<u>Every two weeks,</u>** I eat pizza.	

Unit 3: Key Question and Answer
Q: **How often** do you eat pizza?
A: I eat pizza **twice a month.**

Preparation I

Part 1

Directions: Use an **indefinite frequency adverb** to write sentences about your life.

always
almost always
usually
often
sometimes
occasionally
seldom
rarely
hardly ever
almost never
never

Example

I <u>almost always</u> do my homework.

1) I _____ go to bed late at night.
2) I _____ do my chores.
3) I _____ swim in the ocean.
4) I am _____ late for school.
5) I _____ say please and thank you.
6) _____
   _____

Part 2

Directions: Use a **definite frequency adverb** to write sentences about your life.

Once twice several times ten times	a second/ a minute/ an hour / a day / a week / every two weeks/ a month / a year
every	second / minute / hour / day / week / other week / month / year / five years/ ten years

Example

I brush my teeth <u>every day.</u>

1) I send text messages _____.
2) I exercise _____.
3) _____ I visit the dentist.
4) I eat fast food _____.
5) I cook dinner for my family _____.
6) _____.

Everyday Language Tip

once in a blue moon = very rarely

Ex.
I'm a very healthy person. I only eat fast food **once in a blue moon.**

Preparation II

Directions: Complete the info-gap activity with your partner. Student B goes first: How often does Dylan eat spicy food? Then Student A asks a question

Target Language

Student B: <u>How often</u> does Dylan eat spicy food?

Student A: <u>How often</u> does Suji cook?

No Peeking!

Put a blank piece of paper between these pages so you can't see your partner's information!

A

	eat spicy food	go hiking	watch the news	play phone games	cook
Dylan	almost never		every night		once a day
Alice		occasionally		often	
Rufus	three times a week		rarely		every Monday
Suji		every summer		several times a day	
You					
Ask your partner: How often do you _____ ?					

30

Preparation II

Directions: Complete the info-gap activity with your partner. **Student B goes first: How often does Dylan eat spicy food?** Then Student A asks a question.

Target Language
Student B: <u>How often</u> does Dylan eat spicy food?
Student A: <u>How often</u> does Suji cook?

No Peeking!

Put a blank piece of paper between these pages so you can't see your partner's information!

B

B	eat spicy food	go hiking	watch the news	play phone games	cook
Dylan		every Sunday		occasionally	
Alice	every day		every morning		several times a month
Rufus		never		always	
Suji	sometimes		seldom		almost never
You					

Ask your partner:
How often do you _____?

Preparation III

Directions: Read to your partner, listen, and fill in the blanks.
Student A reads first.

> **No Peeking!**
>
> Put a blank piece of paper between these pages so you can't see your partner's information!

Student A
→ You read, Student B writes

Herman
Herman works at a library. He works five days a week. After work, he usually exercises at the gym. Herman then meets his friends at the coffee shop. He meets his friends once or twice a week. On the weekends, Herman often sees movies at the movie theater. He always gets popcorn and cola. He never orders nachos.

Mary
Mary is an elementary school student. Her favorite subject is math. She does not like art class. She seldom draws or paints pictures. Mary likes to play tag with her friends. She plays tag eight times a month. She also likes to play badminton. Mary's father loves hiking but Mary does not like it. She almost never goes hiking with her father.

→ You write, Student B reads

Darius
Darius is an _____ doctor. He loves animals. Darius has two big dogs. He walks his dogs _____ a day. Darius _____ takes his dogs to the dog park. He also enjoys cooking. Darius cooks delicious food _____. His best recipe is _____ chicken. However, Darius' brother _____ eats spicy food, so Darius _____ cooks hamburgers or _____ for his brother.

Nina
Nina is a pilot. She flies planes _____. Nina enjoys traveling the world and learning new languages. She _____ studies language in the _____. Nina also enjoys listening to music and drinking _____. She _____ listens to music! On the weekends, Nina _____ goes _____ in the park with her friends.

Preparation III

Directions: Read to your partner, listen, and fill in the blanks.
Student A reads first.

> **No Peeking!**
>
> Put a blank piece of paper between these pages so you can't see your partner's information!

Student B
➔ **You write, Student A reads**

Herman
Herman _____ at a library. He works _____ a week. After work, he _____ exercises at the gym. Herman then _____ his friends at the coffee shop. He meets his friends once or _____. On the weekends, Herman _____ sees movies at the movie theater. He _____ gets popcorn and cola. He _____ orders nachos.

Mary
Mary is an elementary school student. Her _____ subject is math. She does not like art class. She _____ draws or paints pictures. Mary likes to play tag with her friends. She _____ tag _____ a _____. She also likes to play badminton. Mary's father loves _____ but Mary does not like it. She _____ goes hiking with her father.

➔ **You read, Student A writes**

Darius
Darius is an animal doctor. He loves animals. Darius has two big dogs. He walks his dogs four times a day. Darius sometimes takes his dogs to the dog park. He also enjoys cooking. Darius cooks delicious food daily. His best recipe is spicy chicken. However, Darius' brother rarely eats spicy food, so Darius occasionally cooks hamburgers or noodles for his brother.

Nina
Nina is a pilot. She flies planes every day. Nina enjoys traveling the world and learning new languages. She usually studies language in the evening. Nina also enjoys listening to music and drinking green tea. She always listens to music! On the weekends, Nina sometimes goes jogging in the park with her friends.

Practice

Directions: Answer the questions with 1-2 sentences. Use a "How often...?" expression in your answer.

Example

How often do you do yoga?
<u>I always do yoga. I do it seven days a week.</u>

① How often do you exercise?

_____

② How often do you clean your room?

_____

③ How often does your family go on vacation?

_____

④ How often do you get 100% on a test?

_____

⑤ How often do you fly a kite?

_____

⑥ How often do you go to the doctor?

_____

⑦ How often do you brush your teeth?

_____

⑧ How often do you get a haircut?

_____

⑨ How often do you have science homework?

_____

⑩ How often do you eat junk food?

_____

Now, write your own "How often..." question and answer it.

Question:_____?

Answer: _____

Everyday Language Tip

Twenty-four seven = always

Ex.
My son is on his smartphone **twenty-four seven**!

Model Conversations

Directions: Read the conversations with your partner. Pay attention to the **Reaction Responses** and **Tell-Me-More Questions**. Add these responses and questions to your notebook.

Reaction Responses	Tell-Me-More Questions
A **Reaction Response** is used to respond or react.	**Tell-Me-More Questions** ask for more information.
Is that right? Seriously? _____ _____ _____	You? Why not? _____ _____ _____

A: How often do you eat eggs for breakfast?

B: I usually eat eggs for breakfast. **You?**

A: I hardly ever eat eggs for breakfast.

B: **Is that right? Why not?**

A: I hate eggs! **You?**

B: **Seriously?** I love eggs!

Directions: Now, fill in the blanks with the **Reaction Responses** and **Tell-Me-More Questions**.

You?   Seriously?   Why not?   Is that right?

A: How often do you sleep late?

B: I occasionally sleep late. _____?

A: I seldom sleep late.

B: _____? _____?

A: Because I start work at 6 a.m., so I have to get up early.

B: _____? That is early!

Text Me

Directions: Create a text conversation with your partner by passing your book back and forth. *No talking!*

A: How often do you _____?

B: _____.

A:

B:

A:

B:

A:

B:

Grade Yourself!		
Level 1	Level 2	Level 3
Conversation Amateur	Conversation Rookie	Conversation Pro
▲ Asks or answers a question	▲ Asks or answers a question ■ Uses a Reaction Response	▲ Asks or answers a question ■ Uses a Reaction Response ★ Asks a Tell-Me-More Question

Real-Life Conversation

Directions: For each question, have a short conversation with Student B. Try to use **Reaction Responses** and **Tell-Me-More Questions** in your conversation.

Student A

- How often do you exercise?
- How often do you clean your room?
- How often does your family go on vacation?
- How often do you get 100% on your English test?
- How often do you fly a kite?
- How often do you read books?
- How often do you go to the dentist?
- How often do you have English class?
- How often do you eat foreign food?
- How often do you travel?
- How often do you go to the shopping mall?

Conversation Checklist

- ○ I <u>asked</u> a question.
- ○ I <u>answered</u> a question.
- ○ I used a **Reaction Response**.
- ○ I asked a **Tell-Me-More-Question**.

Real-Life Conversation

Directions: For each question, have a short conversation with Student A. Try to use **Reaction Responses** and **Tell-Me-More Questions** in your conversation.

Student B

- How often do you go to the doctor?
- How often do you brush your teeth?
- How often do you get a haircut?
- How often are you sick?
- How often do eat junk food?
- How often do you eat eggs for breakfast?
- How often do you stay up past midnight?
- How often do you eat at a restaurant?
- How often do you eat pizza?
- How often do you go to the movies?

Conversation Checklist

- ○ I asked a question.
- ○ I answered a question.
- ○ I used a **Reaction Response**.
- ○ I asked a **Tell-Me-More-Question**.

4. What Are You Going To Do After Class?

Introduction

Be going to + verb is used to indicate **future plans**. It can also be used to make **predictions** about the future.

Plans
- I'm going to talk to my friend.
- It is going to rain this afternoon.

Predictions
- The baby is going to look just like his father.
- I drank too much coffee, so I'm not going to fall asleep tonight.

Affirmative/Negative Statements			
I	am	going to	
You	are		
He	is		
She	is		exercise.
It	is	not	
We	are	going to	
They	are		

Short Answers						or
Yes,		No,				
I	am.	I	am			
you	are.	you	are			aren't.
he	is.	he	is			isn't.
she	is.	she	is	not.	isn't.
it	is.	it	is			isn't.
we	are.	we	are			aren't.
they	are.	they	are			aren't.

Short Answers					or
Yes,		No,			
I	am.	I	am		
you	are.	you	are		
he	is.	he	is		
she	is.	she	is	not.	isn't.
it	is.	it	is		aren't.
we	are.	we	are		
they	are.	they	are		

Information Questions
Where are you going to exercise?
When are you going to exercise?
Why are you going to exercise?
How are you going to exercise? (What exercise are you going to do?)
Who are you going to exercise with?

Answers
I am going to exercise at the gym.
I am going to exercise in the morning.
I am going to exercise for my health.
I am going to do push-ups and sit-ups.
I am going to exercise with Esme.

Unit 4: Key Question and Answer
Q: What **are you going to do** after class?
A: **I am going to exercise** after class.

Preparation I

Directions: Unscramble the sentences.

1. the bus / tomorrow morning / going to / I'm / take

   _____

2. English / study / next semester / Jose / is / going to

   _____

3. next fall / are going to / Washington D.C. / Dan / Tia / and / visit

   _____

4. go sightseeing / this afternoon / My brother and I / are going to / in Paris

   _____

Directions: Complete the sentences using the *future tense with going to*. For 9 and 10, choose your own verbs.

5. (go) I __am going to go__ to the movies this weekend.

6. (play) I _____ smartphone games later.

7. (study) I _____ English tomorrow night.

8. (clean) I _____ my room this afternoon.

★ Challenge ★

9. I _____ at the lake this weekend.

10. My parents _____ me a smartphone for my birthday!

Everyday Language Tip

up in the air = not decided yet

Ex.
My summer vacation plans are still **up in the air**.

Preparation II

Directions: Complete the info-gap activity with your partner. **Partner B goes first** and asks a question about an empty square. Then, **Partner A** asks a question.

Target Language

Student B: What is Vern going to do tonight?
Student A: What is Lilly going to do tomorrow?

A

A	tonight	tomorrow	next weekend	next school vacation	next year
Vern	eat chicken		go fishing		study in Canada
Lilly		study math		learn to cook	
Mike	go to sleep early		play baseball		travel to Europe
Danny		exercise		build a robot	
You					
Ask your partner: What are you going to do _____?					

Preparation II

Directions: Complete the info-gap activity with your partner. **Partner B goes first** and asks a question about an empty square. Then, **Partner A** asks a question.

Target Language

Student B: What is Vern going to do tonight?

Student A: What is Lilly going to do tomorrow?

B

B	tonight	tomorrow	next weekend	next school vacation	next year
Vern		go to school		take singing lessons	
Lilly	bake cookies		stay in a hotel		work in a bank
Mike		read books		work at a coffee shop	
Danny	watch movies		go to an Indian restaurant		graduate from university
You					
Ask your partner: What are you going to do _____?					

Preparation III

Directions: First, complete the chart with your own verbs and time words and answer the questions for yourself. Then, interview your partner and write his or her answer in the space.

←100% Yes, definitely.	75% Probably.	50% Maybe, I'm not sure	25% Probably not.	0% → No way.

Example
A: Are you going to play soccer?
B: Yes, definitely. (100%)
Probably. (75%)
Maybe. I'm not sure. (50%)
Probably not. (25%)
No way. (0%)

			Me	My partner
Example Are you going to	play soccer	tomorrow?	Yes, definitely.	Probably not
Are you going to	exercise			
Are you going to		next week?		
Are you going to	watch a movie	?		
Are you going to		later today?		
Are you going to	drink orange juice	?		
Are you going to		tomorrow morning?		
Are you going to	eat meat	?		
Are you going to		next year?		
Are you going to		on Friday?		
Are you going to	read a novel			
Are you going to	play smartphone games			
Are you going to				
Are you going to				
Are you going to				
Are you going to				

Everyday Language Tip

down the road = sometime in the future

Ex.
Somewhere **down the road**, I'd like to open my own coffee shop.

Practice

Directions: Answer the questions. Use the future tense "be going to."

Example

What homework are you going to do tonight?
I am going to do math homework tonight. After that, I am going to watch TV.

① What are you going to eat for breakfast tomorrow morning?
_____

② What are you going to do next year?
_____

③ What are you going to watch tonight?
_____

④ What are you going to do next school vacation?
_____

⑤ What hobby are you going to do next?
_____

⑥ Do you have any plans for the weekend?
_____

⑦ What are you going to do after class?
_____

⑧ When are you going to go to bed tonight?
_____

⑨ What are you going to study tomorrow?
_____

⑩ What snack are you going to eat this week?
_____

Now, write your own "be going to" question and answer it.

Question:_____?

Answer: _____.

Model Conversations

Directions: Read the conversations with your partner. Pay attention to the **Reaction Responses** and **Tell-Me-More Questions**. Add these responses and questions to your notebook.

A **Reaction Response** is used to respond or react.	**Tell-Me-More Questions** asks for more information.
Really? I think... Maybe I'm not sure. I'm so jealous of you! _____ _____ _____	For how long...? _____ _____ _____ _____

A: What are you going to do next year?

B: I am going to study in Canada.

A: **Really? For how long?**

B: Two years, **I think. I'm not sure.**

A: **I'm so jealous of you.** I really want to go abroad.

B: **What about you?** What are you going to do next year?

A: Nothing special.

> **Remember**
> Keep a list of all the RRs, TMMQs and Everyday Language in your notebook.

Directions: Now, fill in the blanks with the **Reaction Responses** and **Tell-Me-More Questions**.

When...?   Really?   I'm not sure   I'm so jealous of you.

A: Any plans for the weekend?

B: I am going to buy a new smartphone.

A: _____? What kind of smartphone?

B: I am going to get an iPhone or the new Galaxy phone. _____. Which phone is better?

A: Well, the iPhone camera is better.

B: Good advice.

A: _____. I want to get a new phone, too! My smartphone is so old.

B: _____ did you get it?

A: Five years ago.

Text Me

Directions: Create a text conversation with your partner by passing your book back and forth. *No talking!*

A: What are you going to do _____?

B:

A:

B:

A:

B:

A:

B:

Grade Yourself!		
Level 1	**Level 2**	**Level 3**
Conversation Amateur	Conversation Rookie	Conversation Pro
▲ Asks or answers a question	▲ Asks or answers a question ■ Uses a Reaction Response	▲ Asks or answers a question ■ Uses a Reaction Response ★ Asks a Tell-Me-More Question

Real-Life Conversation

Directions: For each question, have a short conversation with Student B. Try to use **Reaction Responses** and **Tell-Me-More Questions** in your conversation.

Student A

- What are you going to eat for breakfast tomorrow morning?
- What are you going to do next year?
- What are you going to watch tonight?
- What are you going to do next school vacation?
- What hobby are you going to do next?
- What book are you going to read next?
- Which subject are you going to study tonight?
- What sport are you going to play this week?
- What errand are you going to do next?
- What are you going to do next Friday?

Conversation Checklist

- I <u>asked</u> a question.
- I <u>answered</u> a question.
- I used a **Reaction Response**.
- I asked a **Tell-Me-More-Question**.

Real-Life Conversation

Directions: For each question, have a short conversation with Student A. Try to use **Reaction Responses** and **Tell-Me-More Questions** in your conversation.

Student B

- Do you have any plans for the weekend?
- What are you going to do after class?
- When are you going to go to bed tonight?
- What are you going to study tomorrow?
- What snack are you going to eat this week?
- What chore are you going to do next?
- Which friend are you going to meet next?
- Which video game are you going to play this weekend?
- What school supplies are you going to buy next?
- What singer/band are you going to listen to today?

Conversation Checklist

- ○ I <u>asked</u> a question.
- ○ I <u>answered</u> a question.
- ○ I used a **Reaction Response**.
- ○ I asked a **Tell-Me-More-Question**.

Everyday Language Review

Directions: Match the Everyday Language with its meaning.

1. couch potato____
2. have a blast____
3. up in the air____
4. hit the books____
5. once in a blue moon____
6. twenty-four seven____
7. down the road____
8. call it a day____

A. have a fun and exciting time
B. very rarely
C. in the future
D. finish work and go home
E. always
F. to study hard
G. not decided yet
H. a lazy person

Check your answers on page 137

Directions: Fill in the blanks with the correct Everyday Language. *Pay attention to verb tense.*

1. Miguel stays inside playing video games and eating snacks all day long! He's such a _____.

2. My family _____ in Paris **last summer**. We saw the Eiffel Tower and visited the Louvre.

3. I usually eat dinner then _____ for two hours before going to bed.

4. My dad's brother lives in Tokyo and he only visits America _____.

5. The new smartphone comes out tomorrow. I've been thinking about it _____.

6. Dan _____ after studying for 8 hours straight.

7. Maria's college plans are still _____. She must decide between Harvard, Yale, and MIT.

8. Maybe _____ I'll start my own business.

Tell-Me-More Question Challenge

Directions: For each statement, complete an appropriate **Tell-Me-More Question**. Make up your own questions for 5 points.

Example

I exercise three times a week.	Points
What exercise do you do?	1
When do you exercise?	2
Who do you exercise with?	3
Why do you exercise?	4
How long do you exercise?	5
Total Points	

I bought a new smartphone last weekend.	Points
What store did you go	1
When did you	2
Who did	3
Why	4
	5
Total Points	

I am going to go to the movies.	Points
What movie are you going to	1
When are you going to	2
Who are you	3
Where	4
	5
Total Points	

Page Total_____

I went out to dinner.	Points
What did you	1
When did	2
Who did	3
Where	4
	5
Total Points	

I like pop music.	Points
Who is your favorite	1
When do you	2
How often	3
Where	4
	5
Total Points	

I am going to buy school supplies.	Points
What are you going to	1
When are you going	2
Where are	3
Who	4
	5
Total Points	

Total Points_____

Reaction Response Practice 1

Directions: Read the dialogues and fill in the blanks with an appropriate **Reaction Response**. Notice all of the *Tell-Me-More Questions* in italics. Can you think of better **Reaction Responses**? You can use your own if you want!

A: What do you like to do?

B: I like to play basketball. *How about you?*

A: I love to sing and dance. *When do you play basketball?*

B: I play basketball every Saturday morning.

A: _____ *How long do you play?*

B: We usually play for 2 or 3 hours.

A: _____

B: *Do you have other hobbies?*

A: I like to write stories. I want to be a writer.

B: _____

A: Did you meet your friends last weekend?

B: Yes, I did.

A: _____ *What did you do?*

B: We played soccer in the park for three hours. *You?*

A: I went to the city with my family.

B: _____ *Where did you go in the city?*

A: We went to the history museum.

B: _____

Part 1 Reaction Responses
1. To say you **understand** or are **interested**: • I see. • Oh yeah? • That's cool. • Really? • Is that right?
2. When you are **unsure**, you can say: • I think… • I'm not sure. • Maybe.
3. To show **surprise**: • Really?!? • Seriously?
4. Your own Reaction Responses: _____ _____ _____ _____ _____ _____ _____ _____ _____

A: How often do you read books?

B: I read books two or three times a week. *You?*

A: I read books every day.

B: _____ *Where do you usually read books?*

A: I usually read books at the bookstore.

B: *What bookstore do you like?*

A: I like Big Books Bookstore in the city.

B: _____ *Are you going there today?*

A: _____ _____

A: What are you going to do after class?

B: I am going to the department store to buy a jacket.

A: _____ *What kind of jacket?*

B: I am going to buy a winter jacket.

A: _____ Have a good time.

B: *What are you going to do after class?*

A: _____ I don't have any plans.

B: _____ *Do you want to come shopping with me?*

A: _____

Part 1 Reaction Responses
1. To show you **understand** or are **interested**:   • I see   • Oh yeah?   • That's cool   • Really?   • Is that right?
2. When you are **unsure**, you can say: • I think…   • I'm not sure   • Maybe
3. To show **surprise**:   • Really?!?   • Seriously?
4. Your own Reaction Responses: _____   _____   _____   _____   _____   _____   _____   _____   _____

Be the Teacher

Level 1 Conversation Amateur	Level 2 Conversation Rookie	Level 3 Conversation Pro
▲ Asks or answers a question	▲ Asks or answers a question ■ Uses a Reaction Response	▲ Asks or answers a question ■ Uses a Reaction Response ★ Asks a Tell-Me-More Question

In this activity, you are the teacher. You will look at example student dialogues and give each one a grade!

Directions:

If the student asks or answers a question draw ▲.

If the student uses a Reaction Response draw ■.

If the student uses a Tell-Me-More Question draw ★.

Example

A: What TV shows do you watch? ▲

B: My favorite TV show is "Infinite Challenge." ▲ *You?* ★

A: I don't really like any TV shows ▲. I just watch the news. ▲

B: I see. ■ *When* do you watch the news? ★

A: I watch the news in the evening. ▲

	▲	■	★	Score
Student A	✓			Level 1 Amateur
Student B	✓	✓	✓	Level 3 Pro

Directions:

If the student asks or answers a question draw ▲.

If the student uses a Reaction Response draw ■.

If the student uses a Tell-Me-More Question draw ★.

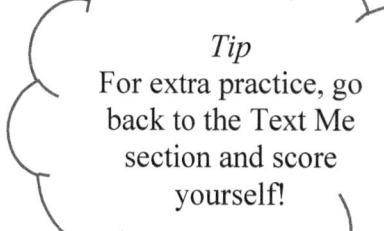

Tip
For extra practice, go back to the Text Me section and score yourself!

A: What did you do last weekend?

B: I got my haircut.

A: *Wow! Looks nice!*

B: Thanks! *What did you do on Sunday?*

A: I visited my grandparents.

B: *Oh yeah? Where did you go* with your grandparents?

A: We went for a walk at the beach and then ate dinner at a seafood restaurant.

B: *Sounds like a good time.*

	▲	■	★	Score
Student A				
Student B				

A: How often do you sleep late?
B: I seldom sleep late.
A: *Really? How come?*
B: Because I start work at 6 a.m., so I have to get up early.
A: *Got it.*

	▲	■	★	Score
Student A				
Student B				

Conversation Test

Part 1

Tip
Record your conversation with a smartphone or other recording device!

Student A

Directions:
Step 1: **Choose 1** question from each unit by marking a ✓
Step 2: **Write 2** of your own questions.
Step 3: Take turns asking and answering the questions (selected and written) with your partner. Remember, each conversation should include **Reaction Responses** and **Tell-Me-More Questions**. Conversations should be at least 8 lines long.
Step 4: Grade your test *(must use a recording device for this step)*.

Unit 1 Choose 1	• What TV shows do you watch? • What do you do in your free time? • What time do you wake up in the morning? • What are two of your hobbies? • What chores do you do at home?	• What do you do before English class? • What do you drink in the morning? • What do you do before school or work? • What do you do before bed? • What activities do you like to do with friends?
Unit 2 Choose 1	• What time did you go to sleep last night? • What TV show did you watch last weekend? • What was the last board game you played? • Who turned out the lights? • What is the last thing you bought?	• What homework did you do last night? • What chore did you do last week? • What was your favorite toy as a child? • Where did you live when you were five years old?
Unit 3 Choose 1	• How often do you exercise? • How often do you clean your room? • How often does your family go on vacation? • How often do you get 100% on your English test? • How often do you fly a kite?	• How often do you read books? • How often do you go to the dentist? • How often do you have English class? • How often do you eat foreign food? • How often do you travel? • How often do you go to the shopping mall?
Unit 4 Choose 1	• What are you going to eat for breakfast tomorrow morning? • What are you going to do next year? • What are you going to watch tonight? • What are you going to do next school vacation? • What hobby are you going to do next?	• What book are you going to read next? • Which subject are you going to study tonight? • What sport are you going to play this week? • What errand are you going to do next? • What are you going to do next Friday?
Your Questions ★	Write two of your own questions 1. _____ 2. _____	

Conversation Test

Part 1

> *Tip*
> Record your conversation with a smartphone or other recording device!

Student B

Directions:
Step 1: Choose 1 question from each unit by marking a ✓
Step 2: Write 2 of your own questions.
Step 3: Take turns asking and answering the questions (selected and written) with your partner. Remember, each conversation should include **Reaction Responses** and **Tell-Me-More Questions**. Conversations should be at least 8 lines long.
Step 4: Grade your test *(must use a recording device for this step)*

Unit 1 Choose 1	●What do you do on the weekends? ●What music do you like to listen to? ●What desserts do you like? ●When do you go to bed at night? ●What exercise do you like to do?	●How do you relax after school or work? ●What kind of foreign food do you like? ●What kind of books do you like to read? ●What do you do after English class? ●What smartphone apps do you use?
Unit 2 Choose 1	●What did you do this morning? ●What did you drink with breakfast? ●What did you do for your last birthday? ●Where did you go on your last school trip? ●What was the last salty snack you ate?	●What did you do on Sunday afternoon? ●What did you eat for dinner last night? ●What was the last wild animal you saw? ●What was the last fruit you ate? ●What was the last sweet thing you ate?
Unit 3 Choose 1	●How often do you go to the doctor? ●How often do you brush your teeth? ●How often do you get a haircut? ●How often are you sick? ●How often do eat junk food?	●How often do you eat eggs for breakfast? ●How often do you stay up past midnight? ●How often do you eat at a restaurant? ●How often do you eat pizza? ●How often do you go to the movies?
Unit 4 Choose 1	●Do you have any plans for the weekend? ●What are you going to do after class? ●When are you going to go to bed tonight? ●What are you going to study tomorrow? ●What snack are you going to eat this week?	●What chore are you going to do next? ●Which friend are you going to meet next? ●Which video game are you going to play this weekend? ●What school supplies are you going to buy next? ●What singer/band are you going to listen to today?
Your Questions ★	Write two of your own questions 1. _____ 2. _____	

Grade Your Test

Directions:
- Choose two conversation questions and record the two conversations.
- Listen to and transcribe your conversations.
- Use the rubric to grade yourself and your partner.

Conversation 1

A: _____

B: _____

A: _____

B: _____

A: _____

B: _____

A: _____

B: _____

A: _____

B: _____

If the student asks or answers a question draw ▲.

If the student uses a Reaction Response draw ■.

If the student uses a Tell-Me-More Question draw ★.

	▲	■	★	Score
Student A				
Student B				

Conversation 2
A: _____
B: _____
A: _____
B: _____
A: _____
B: _____
A: _____
B: _____
A: _____
B: _____

If the student asks or answers a question draw ▲.

If the student uses a Reaction Response draw ■.

If the student uses a Tell-Me-More Question draw ★.

	▲	■	★	Score
Student A				
Student B				

Part 2

5. Because and So

Because and **So** are called conjunctions. Conjunctions are important because they join two ideas together. Because and So are important for conversation because they allow us to speak in longer sentences by adding more details.

Because presents a **reason**	
Winter is my favorite season because I love snow.	*I love snow* is the **reason** winter is my favorite season
I don't like jalapenos because they are too spicy.	*they are too spicy* is the **reason** I don't like jalapenos
Mom is resting because she is tired.	*she is tired* is the **reason** Mom is resting
* because can also come first • Because I love snow, winter is my favorite season. • Because jalapenos are too spicy, I don't like them. • Because she is tired, Mom is resting.	*notice the commas

So presents a **consequence**	
The food is spicy, so I drink some water.	*drinking water* is the **consequence** of eating spicy food
Roberto got 100% on his test, so he was happy.	Roberto's *happiness* is the **consequence** of getting 100% on his test
Nicole is sick, so she is at the doctor's office.	Nicole *going to the doctor* is the **consequence** of her being sick
* notice the comma placed before *so* * so always comes second in a sentence	

Quiz Yourself

Directions: Cover the top half of this paper. Then, answer the questions about BECAUSE and SO.

_____: presents a result or consequence.

Example: We were out of milk, _____ Dennis went to the store to buy some.

_____: presents a reason and answers the question "why?"

Example: Susie was sad _____ she dropped her ice cream on the ground.

Used in conversation, *because* and *so* allow us to give more information to our speaking partner.

more information = even better conversation

From now on, all of your answers should include *because* or *so*!

Preparation I

Directions: Circle BECAUSE or SO.

1. We are tired *(because /, so)* we played soccer for two hours.

2. It is Daniel's birthday *(because /, so)* we are having a birthday party for him.

3. Hawaii has a warm climate *(because /, so)* people usually wear shorts.

4. My desk is messy *(because /, so)* I didn't clean it.

5. Dana got 100% on the English exam *(because /, so)* he studied hard.

6. Neil is sick *(because /, so)* he is taking medicine.

7. I wasn't busy *(because /, so)* I took a nap.

8. My dog wagged his tail *(because /, so)* he was happy.

9. The girls are full *(because /, so)* they ate all of the pizza!

10. Jimmy is hungry *(because /, so)* he will eat a hamburger.

11. I am late for work *(because /, so)* of the bad traffic.

12. It is Christmas *(because /, so)* all the stores are closed.

13. I took my phone to the repair shop *(because /, so)* it was broken.

14. The car stopped *(because /, so)* it was out of gas.

15. It's 2 a.m. *(because /, so)* Max is tired.

Everyday Language Tip

piece of cake = very easy

Ex.
Q: How was the English test?
A: It was a **piece of cake**. I got 100%.

Preparation II

Directions: Complete the sentences with your own ideas.

1A) Al is tired because _____.

1B) Al is tired, so _____.

2A) It is cold outside because _____.

2B) It is cold outside, so _____.

3A) Minny likes soccer because _____.

3B) Minny likes soccer, so _____.

4A) I study English because _____.

4B) I study English, so _____.

5A) John went to the movies because _____.

5B) John went to the movies, so _____.

6A) My favorite season is _____ because _____.

6B) My favorite season is _____, so _____.

Everyday Language Tip

from scratch = from nothing; from the beginning; from basic ingredients

Ex.
Diana built her own technology company **from scratch**.

Practice

Directions: Answer the questions by writing two sentences: one with BECAUSE and one with SO.

Example

What is your favorite season?

BECAUSE: My favorite season is autumn **because** I like the beautiful foliage.

SO: My birthday is in October, **so** autumn is my favorite season.

1. What is your favorite food?

BECAUSE_____.

SO_____.

2. What is your favorite movie?

BECAUSE_____.

SO_____.

3. What is your favorite subject?

BECAUSE_____.

SO_____.

4. What is your favorite fast-food restaurant?

BECAUSE_____.

SO_____.

5. What is your favorite kind of weather?

BECAUSE_____.

SO_____.

6. What is your favorite "Mom's Cooking"?

BECAUSE_____.

SO_____.

7. What is your favorite holiday?

BECAUSE_____.

SO_____.

8. What is your favorite actor or athlete?

BECAUSE_____.

SO_____.

Model Conversations

Directions: Read the conversations with your partner. Pay attention to the **Reaction Responses** and **Tell-Me-More Questions**. Add these responses and questions to your notebook.

Reaction Response	Tell-Me-More Questions
A **Reaction Response** is used to respond or react.	**Tell-Me-More Questions** ask for more information
Got it. Is that so? That's _____. _____ _____	How come? Is that so? _____ _____

A: Who is your favorite superhero?
B: I like Spiderman **because** he wears a cool costume. **You?**
A: I love Batman.
B: **Is that so? How come?**
A: His costume is cool. Also, I love the characters, **so** I have all the comic books, too.
B: **That's interesting.**
A: **How about you?** Do you like comic books, too?
B: No, I like watching superhero movies.
A: Got it.

> **Conversation Tip**
> *How come?* means *Why?*
>
> *How come?* is less formal than *Why?* but is commonly used in everyday conversation.

Directions: Now, fill in the blanks with the **Reaction Responses** and **Tell-Me-More Questions**.

Is that so?   You?   so   How come?   Got it   because

A: What's your favorite snack?

B: I love salty snacks, _____ I love potato chips. _____?

A: Well, I love chocolate but I can't eat it.

B: _____?

A: I don't eat snack food _____ I'm on a diet.

B: _____? Why are you on a diet?

A: I want to lose weight and be healthier.

B: _____.

Text Me

Directions: Create a text conversation with your partner by passing your book back and forth. *No talking!*

A: What is your favorite _____?

B:

A:

B:

A:

B:

A:

B:

Grade Yourself!			
Level 1	**Level 2**	**Level 3**	**Level 4**
Conversation Amateur	Conversation Rookie	Conversation Pro	Conversation Master
▲ Asks or answers a question	▲ Asks or answers a question ■ Uses a Reaction Response	▲ Asks or answers a question ■ Uses a Reaction Response ★ Asks a Tell-Me-More Question	▲ Asks or answers a question ■ Uses a Reaction Response ★ Asks a Tell-Me-More Question ⚡ Uses **because** or **so**

Real-Life Conversation

Directions: For each question, have a short conversation with Student B. Try to use **Reaction Responses, Tell-Me-More Questions** and **because** or **so** in your conversation.

Student A
- What's your favorite food?
- What's your favorite movie?
- What's your favorite subject?
- What's your favorite fast-food restaurant?
- What's your favorite fruit?
- What's your favorite ice cream flavor?
- Who's your favorite band or singer?
- What's your favorite time of day?
- Who's your favorite teacher?
- Who's your best friend?

Conversation Checklist

- I <u>asked</u> a question.
- I <u>answered</u> a question.
- I used a **Reaction Response**.
- I asked a **Tell-Me-More** question.
- I used **because** or **so**.

Real-Life Conversation

Directions: For each question, have a short conversation with Student A. Try to use **Reaction Responses, Tell-Me-More Questions** and **because** or **so** in your conversation.

Student B

- What's your favorite kind of weather?
- What's your favorite "Mom's cooking"?
- What's your favorite holiday?
- Who is your favorite actor or athlete?
- What's your favorite vegetable?
- What's your favorite animal?
- Who's your favorite TV star?
- What's your favorite smell?
- What's your favorite book?
- What's your favorite drink?

Conversation Checklist

- I <u>asked</u> a question.
- I <u>answered</u> a question.
- I used a **Reaction Response**.
- I asked a **Tell-Me-More** question.
- I used **because** or **so**.

6. Which Is More Delicious, Pizza or Broccoli?

Introduction

Comparative Adjectives are used to compare two people, places, or things.

To make a comparison between two nouns, add *–er* to the end of an adjective. If the adjective is long (more than two syllables), add *more* before the adjective. Finally, use *than* before the second noun.

<big>A is _____ than B.</big>
The man is stronger than the boy.
Spaghetti is more delicious than meatloaf.

Two Comparative Question Forms

1. Do you think A is _____ than B?
Example: Do you think math is harder than science?

2. Which is _____, A or B?
Example: Which is harder, math or science?

Adjective	Form	Example	Model Sentence
One syllable and two syllables ending in -y	Adjective + -er Adjective + ier *(first, drop the –y)*	Strong + -er = stronger happy + -ier = happier	The man is **stronger** than the boy. Dogs are **happier** than cats.
Three or more syllables	More + adjective	More delicious	Spaghetti is **more delicious** than meatloaf.

Adjective	Comparative	Opposite
big	bigger	small/smaller
long	longer	short/shorter
hard	harder	easy/easier soft/softer
delicious	more delicious	disgusting/more disgusting
fun	more fun	boring/more boring
rich	richer	poor/poorer
expensive	more expensive	cheap/cheaper
happy	happier	sad/sadder
good	better	bad/worse

<big>Unit 6: Key Question and Answer
Q: Which is more delicious, pizza or broccoli?
A: Pizza is more delicious than broccoli.</big>

Preparation I

Directions: For 1-5, complete the sentences with the correct comparative adjective. For 6-10, write a question for the answer.

1) Which is bigger, a lion or a kitten?

A lion is_____than a_____.

2) Which is longer, a ruler or a pencil?

A ruler is_____.

3) Do you think broccoli is more delicious than pizza?

No. Pizza is more_____than_____.

4) Is it better to be good looking or smart?

I think it is better to be_____than _____.

5) Do you think soccer is more popular than baseball?

I think_____.

Directions: For 6-10, write a question for the answer.

6) Which is sweeter, _____?

A strawberry is sweeter than an apple.

7) Do you think_____?

No, smartphone games are more fun than computer games.

8) _____?

Math is harder than science.

9) _____?

My mom is funnier than my dad.

10) _____?

Cats are cuter than dogs.

Everyday Language Tip

Cost an arm and a leg = very expensive

Ex.
I didn't buy the new iPhone because it **costs an arm and a leg.**

Preparation II

Partner Bingo

Directions: Partners take turns reading sentences to each other. Listen to your partner's sentences and draw an X when you find a sentence on your board. The first player with a line of all Xs is the winner. Want to play longer? Make it 2 or 3 lines to win! A line can be horizontal, vertical, or diagonal.

Read to your Partner:					
Red is prettier than blue.	I agree with you.	A pillow is more comfortable than a rock.	Ice is colder than water.	A giraffe is taller than a turtle.	The sun is brighter than the moon.
Paper is thinner than cardboard.	Potato chips are saltier than carrots.	Cars are faster than bikes.	Driving is more expensive than walking.	A knife is sharper than a spoon.	A brick is heavier than a feather.
I disagree with you.	Do you agree or disagree?	Bread is cheaper than chicken.	Watching TV is more fun than studying math.	Sleeping is easier than exercising.	Summer is warmer than spring.
The flu is worse than a cold.	Dogs are more playful than cats.	Motorcycles are louder than skateboards.	Mountains are higher than hills.	Cookies are sweeter than pretzels.	Wood is softer than metal.

A	Your Bingo Card			
Do you agree or disagree?	Art is easier than science.	Planes are faster than cars.	Birds are louder than ants.
Pillows are softer than rocks.	Broccoli is healthier than pizza.	Textbooks are thicker than notebooks.	I disagree.
Milk is more expensive than water.	Brazil is warmer than Russia.	I agree with you.	A flower is prettier than a rock.
Skyscrapers are taller than schools.	Eating at home is cheaper than eating out.	Clouds are higher than trees.	Stars are brighter than candles.

Preparation II

Partner Bingo

Directions: Partners take turns reading sentences to each other. Listen to your partner's sentences and draw an X when you find a sentence on your board. The first player with a line of all Xs is the winner. Want to play longer? Make it 2 or 3 lines to win! A line can be horizontal, vertical, or diagonal.

Read to your partner:					
A flower is prettier than a rock.	I agree with you.	Sneakers are more comfortable than dress shoes.	Fall is colder than summer.	Skyscrapers are taller than schools.	Stars are brighter than candles.
Textbooks are thicker than notebooks.	Broccoli is healthier than pizza.	Planes are faster than cars.	Milk is more expensive than water.	A needle is sharper than a paper clip.	Elephants are heavier than ducks.
I disagree.	Do you agree or disagree?	Eating at home is cheaper than eating out.	Board games are more fun than smartphone games.	Art is easier than science.	Brazil is warmer than Russia.
Breaking your leg is worse than scraping your knee.	Dolphins are more playful than owls.	Birds are louder than ants.	Clouds are higher than trees.	Sugar is sweeter than salt.	Pillows are softer than rocks.

B	Your Bingo Card		
Dogs are more playful than cats.	Cars are faster than bikes.	I disagree with you.	Cookies are sweeter than pretzels.
Bread is cheaper than chicken.	Mountains are higher than hills.	Motorcycles are louder than skateboards.	The flu is worse than the cold.
The sun is brighter than the moon.	Do you agree or disagree?	Ice is colder than water.	Watching TV is more fun than studying math.
Summer is warmer than spring.	A giraffe is taller than a turtle.	A knife is sharper than a spoon.	Paper is thinner than cardboard.

Preparation III

Step 1: Complete the comparative questions with your own words.
Step 2: Interview your partner with the questions and write his/her answer.
Step 3: Decide whether you agree or disagree with your partner.

Example

fun → more fun	
Which is **more fun**, <u>soccer</u> or <u>baseball</u>?	Partner's answer <u>baseball</u>
Do you **agree** or **disagree** with your partner's answer? (circle one) I totally agree! I agree. I disagree. **(I completely disagree!)**	

delicious → more delicious	
Which is **more delicious**, _____ or _____?	Partner's answer _____
Do you **agree** or **disagree** with your partner's answer? I totally agree! I agree. I disagree. I completely disagree!	

good → better	
Which is **better**, _____ or _____?	Partner's answer _____
Do you **agree** or **disagree** with your partner's answer? I totally agree! I agree. I disagree. I completely disagree!	

interesting → _____

Which is _____, _____ or _____?	Partner's answer _____

Do you **agree** or **disagree** with your partner's answer? **I totally agree!   I agree.   I disagree.   I completely disagree!**

_____ → _____

Which is _____, _____ or _____?	Partner's answer _____

Do you **agree** or **disagree** with your partner's answer? **I totally agree!   I agree.   I disagree.   I completely disagree!**

_____ → _____

Which is _____, _____ or _____?	Partner's answer _____

Do you **agree** or **disagree** with your partner's answer? **I totally agree!   I agree.   I disagree.   I completely disagree!**

Practice

Directions: Answer each question with a comparative adjective.

Example

Which is better, pizza or chicken?
I think chicken is better than pizza.

① Is it better to be rich and ugly or poor and beautiful/handsome?
_____

② Which is tastier, chocolate chip cookies or brownies?
_____

③ Which is more entertaining, playing smartphone games or playing board games?
_____

④ Which is prettier, sunset or sunrise?
_____

⑤ Do you think water or juice is more refreshing?
_____

⑥ Which is better for your health, good diet or regular exercise?
_____

⑦ Do you think English or Spanish is harder?
_____

⑧ Is it better to live in a small house or a big apartment?
_____

⑨ Which is more enjoyable, going to a funny movie or a delicious restaurant?
_____

⑩ Which sport is more fun, soccer or badminton?
_____

★ Write your own comparative question and answer it.

Which is _____, _____ or _____?

Answer: _____.

Everyday Language Tip

go bananas = to celebrate excitedly

Ex.
Dan **went bananas** when the Bears won the Super Bowl.

Model Conversations

Directions: Read the conversations with your partner. Pay attention to the **Reaction Responses** and **Tell-Me-More Questions**. Add these responses and questions to your notebook.

Reaction Responses	Tell-Me-More Questions
A **Reaction Response** is used to respond or react.	**Tell-Me-More Questions** ask for more information.
That's a tough question. I (totally) disagree with you I (completely) agree with you. _____ _____	What do you think? _____ _____

A: Which is more delicious, pizza or chicken?
B: **That's a tough question.**
I think pizza is better than chicken. **What do you think?**
A: Chicken is more delicious than pizza.
B: **I disagree with you.** Pizza is more delicious than chicken.
So, what's your favorite chicken shop?
A: Four Brothers Chicken **because** the chicken is spicy, delicious, and cheap!
B: I can't eat spicy food!
A: **That's too bad!**

> **Remember**
> Keep a list of all the RRs, TMMQs and Everyday Language in your notebook.

Directions: Now, fill in the blanks with the **Reaction Responses** and **Tell-Me-More Questions**.

What do you think?   That's too bad.   so   That's a hard question

A: Is it better to be rich or happy?

B: _____. I'm not sure. _____?

A: I think it is better to be happy than rich.

B: I see. Why do you think that?

A: Being rich doesn't mean you will be happy. There are many sad rich people.

B: Do you know any rich people?

A: Yes, my uncle is a CEO. He's always busy and stressed, _____ he isn't happy.

B: _____.

Text Me

Directions: Create a text conversation with your partner by passing your book back and forth. *No talking!*

A: Which is _____, _____ or _____?

B:

A:

B:

A:

B:

A:

B:

Grade Yourself!			
Level 1	Level 2	Level 3	Level 4
Conversation Amateur	Conversation Rookie	Conversation Pro	Conversation Master
▲ Asks or answers a question	▲ Asks or answers a question ■ Uses a Reaction Response	▲ Asks or answers a question ■ Uses a Reaction Response ★ Asks a Tell-Me-More Question	▲ Asks or answers a question ■ Uses a Reaction Response ★ Asks a Tell-Me-More Question ⚡ Uses **because** or **so**

Real-Life Conversation

Directions: For each question, have a short conversation with Student A. Try to use **Reaction Responses, Tell-Me-More Questions** and **because** or **so** in your conversation.

Student A
- Is it better to be rich and ugly or poor and beautiful/handsome?
- Which is tastier, chocolate cookies or brownies?
- Which is more entertaining, playing smartphone games or playing board games?
- Which is prettier, sunrise or sunset?
- Do you think water or juice is more refreshing?
- Who is a better cook, you or your husband/wife?
- Do you think reading or writing is more interesting?
- Which is more delicious, restaurant food or your mom's cooking?
- Which pet is cuter, a puppy or a kitten?
- Which job is more difficult, a teacher or a chef?

Conversation Checklist

- I <u>asked</u> a question.
- I <u>answered</u> a question.
- I used a **Reaction Response**.
- I asked a **Tell-Me-More** question.
- I used **because** or **so**.

Real-Life Conversation

Directions: Have a short conversation using each question. Try to use the **Reaction Responses** and **Tell-Me-More Questions** in your conversation. Remember, all of your conversations should include **because** or **so**!

Student B

- Which is better for your health, a good diet or regular exercise?
- Do you think English or Spanish is harder?
- Is it better to live in a small house or a big apartment?
- Which is more enjoyable, going to a funny movie or a delicious restaurant?
- Which sport is more fun, soccer or badminton?
- Who is smarter, you or your brother/sister?
- Which is more fun, action movies or animated movies?
- Do you think December or January is colder?
- Which is better, getting 100% on a test or getting $50 for your birthday?
- Who is funnier, Mom or Dad?

Conversation Checklist

- I asked a question.
- I answered a question.
- I used a **Reaction Response**.
- I asked a **Tell-Me-More** question.
- I used **because** or **so**.

7. What Animal Is The Cutest?

Introduction

Superlative adjectives are used to compare a person or thing with every other person or thing in a group.

Superlative Adjective Rules

1) One syllable adjectives: the + adjective + -est

    He is the **tallest** member of his family.

2) Two or more syllable adjectives: the + most + adjective

    This iPhone is the **most expensive** phone in the store.

3) Two-syllable adjectives ending in y: drop the y and add -iest

    She is the *funniest* person here.

4) To show the opposite, use **least** instead of **most**.

The iPhone is the *most expensive* phone. → The iPhone is the *least expensive* phone.

5) Be careful! There are some exceptions:
    good (best), bad (worst), far (furthest/farthest), and many others.

Unit 7: Key Question and Answer
Q: What animal is **the cutest**?
A: (I think) The monkey is **the cutest** animal.

Preparation I

Directions: Fill in the blanks with the correct adjective form.

Adjective	Comparative	Superlative
	bigger	biggest
tall		tallest
small	smaller	
	easier	
hard		hardest
strong		
spicy		
		prettiest
	longer	
handsome		
rich		
happy		happiest
		most fun
	more delicious	
expensive		
	more intelligent	
famous		most famous
		best
	worse	

Everyday Language Tip

top-notch = the highest quality, excellent

Ex.
Tino is a straight-A student and a **top-notch** high school wrestler.

83

Preparation II

Finish	kindest person	Ask a ?	Name a restaurant that is second to none. hint: look on page 87!
	Directions: Roll the dice, move to the space, and make a sentence using the **superlative adjective**.		**Move ahead 2**
most boring subject	Ask a ?	most creative person	shortest friend
Ask a ?		**If you agree…** Yes, I totally agree! You can say that again!	
Name a top-notch athlete.	**Roll Again**	funniest family member	hardest subject
	Question Examples ◇ Who is the <u>oldest person</u> in your family? ◇ Which vegetable is <u>least delicious</u>?		**Miss a Turn**
busiest day of the week	least exciting sport	ugliest color	richest person
Ask a ?	**If you disagree…** I totally disagree! Get out of here! No way!		
most interesting job	wisest person	worst vacation destination	most refreshing drink
Superlative Adjectives			Start

84

Preparation III

Directions: First, fill in the blanks with the appropriate choices. Then, take turns interviewing your partner. *Keep the conversation going with **Reaction Responses, Tell-Me-More Questions**, and **Because** and **So**.*

Student A

Which animal is the **happiest**?
- A. dog
- B. cat
- C. rabbit
- D. monkey

Which product is the **most expensive**?
- A. _____
- B. _____
- C. _____
- D. _____

Which is the **prettiest**?
- A. _____
- B. _____
- C. _____
- D. _____

Which drink is the **most refreshing**?
- A. _____
- B. _____
- C. _____
- D. _____

Which character is the **scariest**?
- A. _____
- B. _____
- C. _____
- D. _____

Write your own question!

Which _____ is the _____?
- A.
- B.
- C.
- D.

Preparation III

Directions: First, fill in the blanks with appropriate choices. Then, take turns interviewing your partner. *Keep the conversation going with **Reaction Responses, Tell-Me-More Questions,** and **Because** and **So.***

Student B

Which activity is **most fun**?
- A. playing smartphone games
- B. playing soccer
- C. going fishing
- D. riding a bike

Which animal is the **strongest**?
- A. _____
- B. _____
- C. _____
- D. _____

Which season is the **best**?
- A. _____
- B. _____
- C. _____
- D. _____

Which subject is the **hardest**?
- A. _____
- B. _____
- C. _____
- D. _____

Which illness is the **worst**?
- A. _____
- B. _____
- C. _____
- D. _____

Write your own question!

Which _____ is the _____?
- A.
- B.
- C.
- D.

Practice

Directions: Answer the questions using superlative adjectives.

Example

What is the most refreshing drink?
I think Coke is the most refreshing drink.

① What is the cutest animal?
___

② What is the spiciest food?
___

③ What is the sourest fruit?
___

④ What is the best city in the world?
___

⑤ What is the funniest movie?
___

⑥ What's your mom's most delicious recipe?
___

⑦ What's the most popular place to visit in your country?
___

⑧ What is the best show on TV?
___

⑨ What is the most interesting subject at school?
___

⑩ What is the most exciting game?
___

Write and answer your own superlative question.

___?

___.

Everyday Language Tip

second to none = the best

Ex.
My grandma's homemade banana bread is **second to none!**

87

Model Conversations

Directions: Read the conversations with your partner. Pay attention to the **Reaction Responses** and **Tell-Me-More Questions**. Add these responses and questions to your notebook.

Reaction Responses	Tell-Me-More Questions
A **Reaction Response** is used to respond or react.	**Tell-Me-More Questions** ask for more information.
Totally! Great idea. Good call! = Good idea! Yes! Totally! You can say that again! No way! Get out of here! Couldn't agree more. _____ _____	What's your opinion? _____ _____

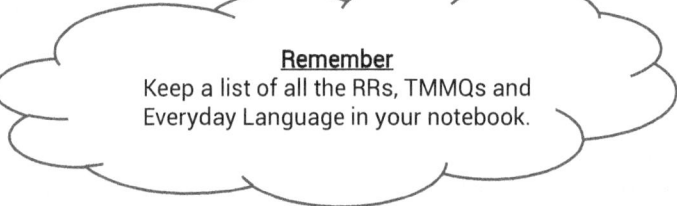

Remember
Keep a list of all the RRs, TMMQs and Everyday Language in your notebook.

A: Wow! It's hot today. I need something cold to drink.
B: **Totally!** Let's go to the convenience store.
A: **Great idea.** What's the **most refreshing** drink?
B: Hmmm, I think ice-cold cola is the most refreshing drink because it has a lot of bubbles. **What's your opinion?**
A: **Couldn't agree more!** Let's buy two ice cold colas!
B: **Good call!**

Directions: Now, fill in the blanks with the **Reaction Responses** and **Tell-Me-More Questions.**

What's your opinion?   Great idea!   Couldn't agree more   Totally!   Good call!

A: Hey Susie! I'm thinking of getting a pet.
B: Really? _____!
A: Yep, I love animals. Which pet is the cutest?
B: I think dogs are the cutest because of their cute eyes and ears. _____?
A: _____. Puppies are so cute!
B: Let's go to the pet store together.
A: _____.

88

Text Me

Directions: Create a text conversation with your partner by passing your book back and forth. *No talking!*

A: What _____ is _____?

B:

A:

B:

A:

B:

A:

B:

Grade Yourself!			
Level 1	**Level 2**	**Level 3**	**Level 4**
Conversation Amateur	Conversation Rookie	Conversation Pro	Conversation Master
▲ Asks or answers a question	▲ Asks or answers a question ■ Uses a Reaction Response	▲ Asks or answers a question ■ Uses a Reaction Response ★ Asks a Tell-Me-More Question	▲ Asks or answers a question ■ Uses a Reaction Response ★ Asks a Tell-Me-More Question ⚡ Uses **because** or **so**

Real-Life Conversation

Directions: For each question, have a short conversation with Student B. Try to use **Reaction Responses, Tell-Me-More Questions** and **because** or **so** in your conversation.

Student A
- What is the cutest animal?
- What is the spiciest food?
- What is the sourest fruit?
- What is the best city in the world?
- What is the funniest movie?
- Who is the kindest person you know?
- Who is the oldest person in your family?
- Which month is the hottest in your country?
- Who is the wisest person you know?
- Where is the best place to go on vacation?

Conversation Check-List

O I <u>asked</u> a question.

O I <u>answered</u> a question.

O I used a **Reaction Response**.

O I asked a **Tell-Me-More Question**.

O I used **because** or **so**.

Real-Life Conversation

Directions: For each question, have a short conversation with Student A. Try to use **Reaction Responses, Tell-Me-More Questions** and **because** or **so** in your conversation.

Student B
- What's your mom's most delicious recipe?
- What's the most popular place to visit in your country?
- What is the best show on TV?
- What is the most interesting subject to study?
- What is the most exciting game?
- Who is the most creative person you know?
- What is the coolest car?
- What is the most disgusting food?
- What is the most boring subject in school?
- Which month is the coldest in your country?

Conversation Check-List
O I <u>asked</u> a question.

O I <u>answered</u> a question.

O I used a **Reaction Response**.

O I asked a **Tell-Me-More Question**.

O I used **because** or **so**.

8. Which Do You Prefer, Soccer or Basketball?

Introduction

Prefer means to **like one** thing more than another.

Example
Q: Do you prefer pizza or chicken?
A: I prefer **chicken** to **pizza.**

In this above example, the person likes chicken **more than** pizza.

Question Structure
- Do you prefer <u>A</u> or <u>B</u>? Do you prefer pizza or chicken?
- Which do you prefer, <u>A</u> or <u>B</u>? Which do you prefer, pizza or chicken?

Answer Structure
- I prefer <u>A</u> to <u>B</u>. I prefer chicken to pizza.
- I like <u>A</u> more than <u>B</u>. I like chicken more than pizza.

Why?
1. *Why?* is a great Tell-Me-More Question to use with a preference question.
2. You can answer *why?* with **because** and then explain it with *so, a comparative adjective,* or *a superlative adjective.*

Example 1
Q: Do you prefer pizza or chicken?
A: I prefer chicken to pizza.
Q: *Why?*
A: I prefer chicken <u>because</u> I think it is *tastier* than pizza.

Example 2
Q: Do you prefer pizza or chicken?
A: I prefer chicken to pizza.
Q: *Why?*
A: Chicken is the most delicious food, so I eat it all the time!

Unit 8: Key Question and Answer
Q: **Which do you prefer**, soccer or basketball?
A: I **prefer** soccer to basketball.

Preparation I

Directions: The answer is provided. Write the question.

1) Question: _____?

Answer: I prefer coffee to tea.

2) Question: _____?

Answer: I prefer warm weather to cold weather.

Directions: Answer the questions.

3) Question: Which do you prefer, smartphones or tablets?

Answer: _____.

4) Question: Do you prefer hiking on a mountain or swimming in the ocean?

Answer: _____.

Directions: Add information after **because** and **so**.

5.
Q: Do you prefer summer or winter?
A: I prefer winter to summer.
Q: *Why?*
A: I like winter because _____.

6.
Q: Do you prefer Italian food or Chinese food?
A: I prefer Italian food.
Q: *Why?*
A: I love tomato sauce and cheese, so _____.

7.
Q: Do you prefer dogs or cats?
A: I like dogs more than cats.
Q: *Why is that?*
A: Dogs are better because _____.

Preparation II

Directions: First, complete the chart with your own preferences. Then, interview your partner and write the answer on the line. For #17, write your own question.

	Me	Partner	
1. Do you prefer pizza or chicken?			
2. Do you prefer dogs or cats?			
3. Do you prefer winter vacation or summer vacation?			
4. Do you prefer computer games or smartphone games?			
5. Do you prefer riding the bus or the train?			
6. Do you prefer eating at home or eating at a restaurant?			
7. Do you prefer cold weather or hot weather?			
8. Do you prefer watching movies at home or at the movie theater?			
9. Do you prefer giving presents or getting presents?			
10. Do you prefer ping-pong or bowling?			
11. Do you prefer standing up or sitting down?			
12. Do you prefer apples or oranges?			
13. Do you prefer a delicious breakfast or a delicious dinner?			
14. Do you prefer Mom's cooking or fast food?			
15. Do you prefer Batman or Spiderman?			
16. Do you prefer coffee or tea?			
17. Do you prefer _____ or _____?			

How many answers are the same? _____

13-17: BFFs   *8-12: Buddies*   *7 or less: Strangers*

Everyday Language Tip

in the blink of an eye = very quickly

Ex.
When I order pepperoni pizza, I eat it **in the blink of an eye**.

Preparation III

Flick and Speak

5 points	I prefer ____ to orange juice.	I prefer winter to ____.	I prefer ____ to Monday because ____.	I prefer rainy weather to ____.
4 points	I prefer dogs to ____, so ____.	Steal 5 points from your partner!	I prefer ____ to comedy movies.	I prefer ____ to fast food because ____.
3 points	I prefer spaghetti to ____.	I prefer ____ to reading books because ____.	I prefer ____ to going to the movies.	Switch points with your partner!
2 points	Both teams lose ALL points!	I prefer milk to ____.	I prefer pizza to ____, so ____.	I prefer ____ to soccer.
1 point	I prefer ____ to swimming.	I prefer fall to ____ because ____.	I prefer ____ to math.	I prefer bananas to ____.

Scoreboard

Player	Points
1	
2	

Put coin here.

Directions
① Flick the coin to a space.
② Make a sentence using the information in the space.
③ If you say the sentence correctly, get the points.
④ Once a sentence is said correctly, draw an X on the space. This space is now unplayable.
⑤ The player with the most points at the end is the winner!

Practice

Directions: Answer each question with the **I prefer A to B** sentence pattern.

Example
Do you prefer Iron Man or Captain America?

I prefer Iron Man to Captain America.

① Do you prefer a banana or watermelon?
_____

② Do you prefer running or riding a bike?
_____

③ Do you prefer reading or writing?
_____

④ Which do you prefer, watching the news or reading the news?
_____

⑤ Do you prefer hot drinks or cold drinks?
_____

⑥ Do you prefer spaghetti or steak?
_____

⑦ Do you prefer monkeys or rabbits?
_____

⑧ Which do you prefer, soccer or basketball?
_____

⑨ Do you prefer action movies or comedy movies?
_____

Write and answer your own preference question.

Do you prefer _____ or _____?

Answer: _____.

Everyday Language Tip

on the same page = in agreement

Ex.
A: I prefer to relax on vacation.
B: We're **on the same page**. I prefer lying on the beach to sightseeing in the busy city.

Model Conversations

Directions: Read the conversations with your partner. Pay attention to the **Reaction Responses** and **Tell-Me-More Questions**. Add these responses and questions to your notebook.

Reaction Responses	Tell-Me-More Questions
A **Reaction Response** is used to respond or react.	**Tell-Me-More Questions** ask for more information
Good question. Bingo! (= you're right!!) _____ _____	You? What/When/Where/Why did you ____?

Model Conversations

Directions: Read the conversations with your partner. Pay attention to the **Reaction Responses** and **Tell-Me-More Questions**. Add these responses and questions to your notebook.

A: Do you prefer PE or lunchtime?
B: **Good question.** I prefer PE to lunchtime **because** PE is my favorite subject.
A: Can you guess which one I prefer?
B: Hmm, let me think. Lunch?
A: **Bingo!** I love to eat, **so** I prefer lunchtime to PE. **What did you do** in PE today?
B: We played dodgeball. It was great! **What did you** have for lunch?
A: I ate chicken soup, a sandwich, and a salad. It was delicious.

Directions: Now, fill in the blanks with the **Reaction Responses** and **Tell-Me-More Questions**.

Where did you...?   so   Good question   Bingo

A: Do you prefer eating at home or eating in a restaurant?
B: _____. I prefer eating at home. You?
A: Can you guess?
B: I think you like eating at a restaurant more than eating at home.
A: _____!
B: Why?
A: My mom isn't a good cook, _____ I prefer eating at a restaurant. Don't tell her I said that!
B: Don't worry! Your secret is safe with me. _____ eat lunch?
A: I ate at McDonald's.

97

Text Me

Directions: Create new conversations with your partner. No talking!

A: Do you prefer _____ or _____?

B: _____

A:

B:

A:

B:

A:

B:

Grade Yourself!			
Level 1	Level 2	Level 3	Level 4
Conversation Amateur	Conversation Rookie	Conversation Pro	Conversation Master
▲ Asks or answers a question	▲ Asks or answers a question ■ Uses a Reaction Response	▲ Asks or answers a question ■ Uses a Reaction Response ★ Asks a Tell-Me-More Question	▲ Asks or answers a question ■ Uses a Reaction Response ★ Asks a Tell-Me-More Question ⚡ Uses **because** or **so**

Real-Life Conversation

Directions: For each question, have a short conversation with Student B. Try to use **Reaction Responses, Tell-Me-More Questions** and **because** or **so** in your conversation.

Student A

- Do you prefer spaghetti or steak?
- Do you prefer monkeys or rabbits?
- Which do you prefer, soccer or basketball?
- Do you prefer action movies or comedy movies?
- Do you prefer spring or fall?
- Do you prefer dogs or cats?
- Do you prefer computer games or smartphone games?
- Do you prefer riding the bus or riding the train?
- Which do you prefer, eating at home or eating at a restaurant?
- Do you like cold weather or hot weather?

Conversation Checklist

- I asked a question.
- I answered a question.
- I used a **Reaction Response**.
- I asked a **Tell-Me-More** question.
- I used **because** or **so**.

Real-Life Conversation

Directions: For each question, have a short conversation with Student A. Try to use **Reaction Responses, Tell-Me-More Questions** and **because** or **so** in your conversation.

Student B
- Do you prefer a banana or watermelon?
- Do you prefer running or riding a bike?
- Do you prefer reading or writing?
- Which do you prefer, watching the news or reading the news?
- Do you prefer hot drinks or cold drinks?
- Do you prefer giving presents or getting presents?
- Which do you prefer, standing up or sitting down?
- Do you prefer fast food or Mom's home cooking?
- Do you prefer working in a group or working alone?
- Do you prefer yoga or weightlifting?

Conversation Checklist

- I <u>asked</u> a question.
- I <u>answered</u> a question.
- I used a **Reaction Response**.
- I asked a **Tell-Me-More** question.
- I used **because** or **so**.

9. What Country Should I Visit?

Introduction

Should is used to ask for and give advice. It can be used for asking questions, and giving negative and positive advice.

Question
- ✓ Where **should** we eat dinner?
- ✓ **Should** I see the new Marvel movie?
- ✓ **Should** he go abroad next year?

Negative Advice
- ✓ You **should not** eat too much sugar.
- ✓ He **shouldn't** run in the house.
- ✓ They **shouldn't** talk in the library.

Positive Advice
- ✓ You **should** wear a heavy winter coat.
- ✓ He **should** try the bulgogi pizza.
- ✓ They **should** hike to the top of the mountain.

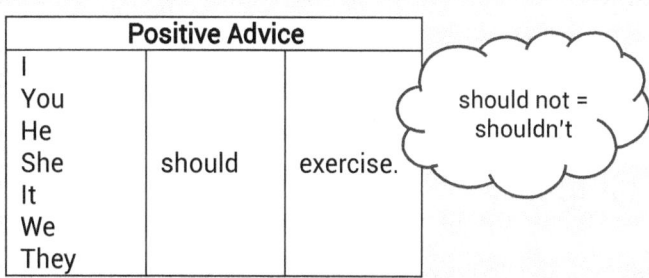

Positive Advice		
I You He She It We They	should	exercise.

should not = shouldn't

Negative Advice		
I You He She It We They	shouldn't	exercise.

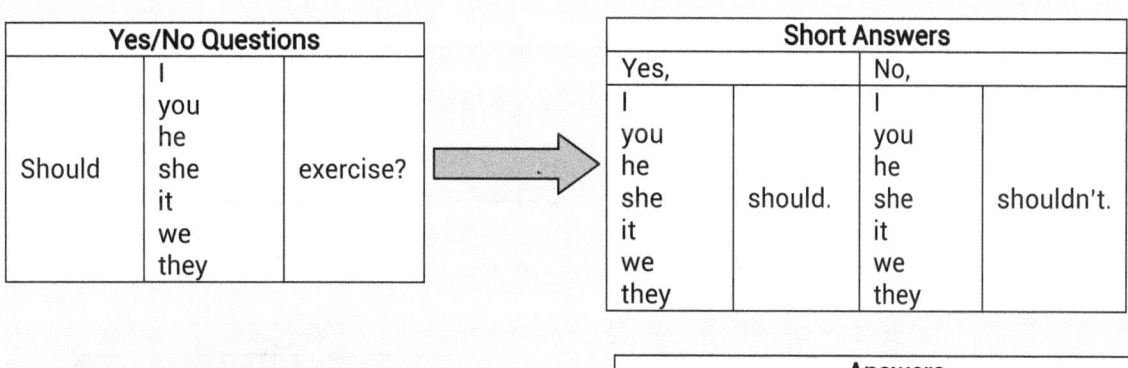

Yes/No Questions		
Should	I you he she it we they	exercise?

Short Answers				
Yes,			No,	
I you he she it we they	should.		I you he she it we they	shouldn't.

Information Questions
What exercise should I do?
Where should I go grocery shopping?
When should I wake up tomorrow?
Why should I see the doctor?
How often should I see the dentist?

Answers
You should do Pilates.
You should go to Big Mart.
You should wake up at 5 a.m.
You should see the doctor because you are sick.
You should see the dentist every six months.

Unit 9: Key Question and Answer
Q: What country **should** I visit?
A: You **should** visit Korea.

Preparation I

Directions: Give advice using some of the expressions below, using should or shouldn't.

~~study more~~	save money	exercise	wake up earlier
eat too much candy	visit the Statue of Liberty	buy a birthday present	take some medicine
eat a lot of fast food	wear a seatbelt	travel abroad	use (my) smartphone

Example

I got a low score on my English test.
You should study more.

1. I am riding in the car with my cousin.

_____.

2. I really want to buy new shoes but I don't have enough money!

_____.

3. The doctor told me I should try to lose weight.

_____.

4. I want to learn about different cultures and meet new people.

_____.

5. I am sitting in the movie theater. The movie is starting now.

_____.

6. I went to the dentist. I have three cavities.

_____.

Everyday Language Tip

under the weather = sick, ill

Ex.
A: I'm feeling a little **under the weather**. What should I do?
B: Take this medicine and take a nap.

Preparation II

Student A

Part 1

Directions: Say these sentences to your partner. Your partner will respond.

1. I have a terrible toothache! What should I do?
2. The news said there will be a storm later today. What should I do?
3. My smartphone is broken. What should I do?
4. I am always late for school.
5. I want to improve my English speaking.

Part 2

Directions: Now, listen to your partner's questions. Choose the best responses. There may be more than one good answer!

1.
   - A. You should go to the dentist.
   - B. You should buy some dog food.
   - C. You should go to the animal doctor.
   - D. You shouldn't play with your dog.
   - E. You should take your dog outside.

2.
   - A. You shouldn't play soccer.
   - B. You should make a birthday cake.
   - C. You should brush your teeth.
   - D. You should go to the grocery store.
   - E. You shouldn't go to the movies with your friends.

3.
   - A. You shouldn't do homework.
   - B. You should exercise more.
   - C. You should drink some cold water.
   - D. You should take a nap.
   - E. You shouldn't take a shower.

4.
   - A. You should run.
   - B. You shouldn't wait for another bus.
   - C. You should go home.
   - D. You shouldn't text your friend.
   - E. You should call a taxi.

5.
   - A. You should eat a snack.
   - B. You shouldn't play smartphone games.
   - C. You should talk to your teacher.
   - D. You should study hard.
   - E. You should buy a new notebook.

Preparation II

Student B

Part 1

Directions: Listen to your partner. Choose the best responses. There may be more than one good answer!

1.
    A. You should buy a new sweater.
    B. You should brush your teeth.
    C. You should go see the dentist.
    D. You should eat ice cream.
    E. You shouldn't watch too much TV.

2.
    A. You shouldn't watch the news.
    B. You shouldn't eat lunch.
    C. You should bring an umbrella.
    D. You shouldn't go outside.
    E. You should wear warm clothes.

3.
    A. You should go to the phone repair shop.
    B. You shouldn't play phone games.
    C. You should be careful.
    D. You should buy a new smartphone.
    E. You should read more often.

4.
    A. You should do your homework.
    B. You shouldn't stay up too late.
    C. You should take the bus to school.
    D. You should use an alarm clock in the morning.
    E. You should go to summer school.

5.
    A. You shouldn't read books.
    B. You practice study math and science.
    C. You should travel a lot.
    D. You should meet friends from other countries.
    E. You should watch Spiderman.

Part 2

Directions: Say these sentences to your partner. Your partner will respond.

1. My dog is sick. What should I do?
2. It is my mom's birthday today. What should I do?
3. I just exercised for one hour. What should I do?
4. I missed the bus. What should I do?
5. I failed the history test. What should I do?

Preparation III

You Should Guess!

Directions: Make lists of places you often, sometimes, rarely, and never visit. For example, *grocery store* should be in the ***often*** column.

I **often** visit...	I **sometimes** visit...	I **rarely** visit...	I **never** visit...
1.	1.	1.	1.
2.	2.	2.	2.
3.	3.	3.	3.

Game Rules

- Now, choose one place from each column. Don't show your partner!
- Write three **should** or **shouldn't** sentences about each place.
- Then, read the sentences to your partner. He/she should guess each place.

Example

Round 1: Often (1 point)	
Place	School
1. You should bring a pencil.	
2. You shouldn't bring your smartphone.	
3. You should study a lot.	
My partner was	○ Correct! ○ Incorrect!

Round 1: Often (1 point)

Place	
1.	
2.	
3.	
My partner was	○ Correct! ○ Incorrect!

Tip

Write difficult clues so it is hard for your partner to guess!

Round 2: Sometimes (2 points)

Place	
1.	
2.	
3.	
My partner was	○ Correct! ○ Incorrect!

Round 3: Rarely (3 points)

Place	
1.	
2.	
3.	
My partner was	○ Correct! ○ Incorrect!

Round 4: Never (4 points)

Place	
1.	
2.	
3.	
My partner was	○ Correct! ○ Incorrect!

Partner's Total Points _____

Practice

Directions: Answer the questions about your own life. Use "should."

Example

Should I order the chicken or the spaghetti?
You **should** order the chicken. It's super delicious.

① What healthy foods should I eat?

_____

② I want to have an adventurous vacation. Where should I go?

_____

③ I am visiting your hometown next weekend. Suggest a delicious restaurant for me.

_____

④ What are two things a person should do to be rich?

_____

⑤ Should elementary school students study a foreign language?

_____

⑥ Should children have smartphones?

_____

⑦ What movie should I watch next weekend?

_____

⑧ Suggest a great book for me to read.

_____

⑨ What pizza toppings should I order?

_____

⑩ How often should I exercise?

_____

Write and answer your own *should* question.

_____?
_____.

Everyday Language Tip

health nut = a person who enjoys a very healthy lifestyle

Ex.
Derek is a **health nut**. He doesn't eat red meat and exercises two hours a day.

Model Conversations

Directions: Read the conversations with your partner. Pay attention to the **Reaction Responses** and **Tell-Me-More Questions**. Add these responses and questions to your notebook.

Reaction Responses	Tell-Me-More Questions
A **Reaction Response** is used to respond or react.	**Tell-Me-More Questions** ask for more information
I'm sorry to hear that. I think… Sounds good to me. _____ _____	How about _____? What should I do? _____ _____

> **Remember**
> Keep a list of all the RRs, TMMQs and Everyday Language in your

A: I am super stressed-out these days.
B: Oh, **I'm sorry to hear that.**
A: **What should I do?**
B: **I think** you should start exercising and going to bed earlier. Also, you shouldn't eat too much junk food and fast food. You know?
A: Yeah, you're probably right.
B: By the way, I'm going to meet some friends. **How about** playing some soccer now?
A: **Sounds good to me!**

Directions: Now, fill in the blanks with the **Reaction Responses** and **Tell-Me-More Questions**.

How about…?   I think   What should I do?   I'm sorry to hear that   Sounds good to me

A: I have a terrible stomachache. _____?

B: _____. I think you should take some medicine.

A: I took some medicine but I still feel sick. Should I take more medicine?

B: No, you shouldn't take too much medicine.

A: Any ideas?

B: Yes, I have a good idea. _____ drinking some ginger tea? _____ it will make your stomach feel better.

A: _____.

Text Me

Directions: Create new conversations with your partner by passing your book back and forth. No talking!

A: What should I _____?

B: _____

A: _____

B: _____

A: _____

B: _____

A: _____

B: _____

Grade Yourself!			
Level 1	Level 2	Level 3	Level 4
Conversation Amateur	Conversation Rookie	Conversation Pro	Conversation Master
▲ Asks or answers a question	▲ Asks or answers a question ■ Uses a Reaction Response	▲ Asks or answers a question ■ Uses a Reaction Response ★ Asks a Tell-Me-More Question	▲ Asks or answers a question ■ Uses a Reaction Response ★ Asks a Tell-Me-More Question ⚡ Uses **because** or **so**

Real-Life Conversation

Directions: For each question, have a short conversation with Student B. Try to use **Reaction Responses**, **Tell-Me-More Questions** and **because** or **so** in your conversation.

Student A
- What healthy foods should I eat?
- I want to have an adventurous vacation. Where should I go?
- I am visiting your hometown next weekend. Suggest a delicious restaurant.
- What are two things a person should do to be rich?
- Should elementary school students study a foreign language?
- What should you do when there is an earthquake?
- I am visiting America next week. Where should I go?
- I have a terrible cold. What should I do?
- There is a strong storm coming this way. What should I do?
- I want to live in another country for one year. Where should I move?

Conversation Checklist

- ○ I <u>asked</u> a question.
- ○ I <u>answered</u> a question.
- ○ I used a **Reaction Response**.
- ○ I asked a **Tell-Me-More** question.
- ○ I used **because** or **so**.

Real-Life Conversation

Directions: For each question, have a short conversation with Student A. Try to use **Reaction Responses, Tell-Me-More Questions** and **because** or **so** in your conversation.

Student B

- Should children have smartphones?
- What movie should I watch next weekend?
- Suggest a great book for me to read.
- What pizza toppings should I order?
- How often should I exercise?
- What should you do when there is a fire?
- What are two things a person should do to be healthy?
- I lost my smartphone. What should I do?
- I found a twenty-dollar bill on the street. What should I do?
- My friend hates spicy food. What foreign food should we eat?

Conversation Checklist

- ○ I <u>asked</u> a question.
- ○ I <u>answered</u> a question.
- ○ I used a **Reaction Response**.
- ○ I asked a **Tell-Me-More** question.
- ○ I used **because** or **so**.

10. If It Rains, What Will You Do?

Introduction

The **first conditional** is used to talk about what might happen in the future.

Examples
- If it rains, I won't play soccer outside.
- If I have enough money, I'll buy a new smartphone.
- He will miss the train if he doesn't leave at 9:00 a.m.

will not = won't

\	First Conditional Structure	
	You can write the first conditional in two ways:	
If goes <u>first</u>	If I catch a cold,	I **will see** the doctor..
If goes <u>second</u>*	I **will see** the doctor	if I catch a cold.
	*no comma when *if* goes <u>second</u>	

You try:		
If goes <u>first</u>	If it rains,	_____.
If goes <u>second</u>	I won't play soccer	<u>if </u>.

Unit 10: Key Question and Answer
Q: **If** it rains this weekend, what **will** you do?
A: **If it rains this weekend, I will stay home** and **watch movies**.
or
A: **I will stay home and watch movies if** it rains this weekend.

Preparation I

Directions: Complete the sentences with the verbs in brackets.

Example: <u>If you (not eat) breakfast, you (be) hungry.</u>
<u>If you don't eat breakfast, you will be hungry.</u>

1. If I (not study) for the English test, I (not get) a high score.
   _____.

2. I (go) to the movies if it (rain) this weekend.
   _____.

3. I (buy) a new smartphone if I (save) enough money.
   _____.

4. If we (go) out to dinner tonight, we (go) to an Italian restaurant.
   _____.

5. I (meet) my sister at the coffee shop if she (call) me later.
   _____.

Directions: Complete each sentence with an appropriate beginning or ending.

Example: <u>If it snows, we'll make a snowman.</u>

6. <u>If I don't exercise,</u> _____.

7. <u>If Mike gets a high score on the test,</u> _____.

8. <u>They will get wet if</u> _____.

9. <u>She will laugh if</u> _____.

10. _____, I will be late.

Preparation II

First Conditional Oral Dictation

Directions: Read the sentence stems to your partner. Your partner will complete the sentence using the first conditional and a comma if necessary. Write your partner's response on the line.

Student A

1. If the weather is nice,

   _____.

2. I will swim in the ocean if

   _____.

3. If I go to the Italian restaurant,

   _____.

4. I will play soccer with my friends if

   _____.

5. If I get up early tomorrow,

   _____.

6. I will be hungry if

   _____.

Everyday Language Tip

over the moon = very happy

Ex.
Viviana gave birth to a healthy baby girl. Her family is **over the moon!**

Preparation II
First Conditional Oral Dictation

Directions: Read the sentence stems to your partner. Your partner will complete the sentence using the first conditional and a comma if necessary. Write your partner's response on the line.

Student B

1. I will be angry if
_____.

2. If I go to Tokyo next week,
_____.

3. If I win the contest,
_____.

4. If it snows tomorrow,
_____.

5. I will feel better if
_____.

6. Our teacher will be happy if
_____.

Preparation III

All Done!	I will be over the moon if _____.	Do ten jumping jacks!	I will watch the news tonight if…
Directions: Roll the dice and finish the sentences using the **first conditional tense.**			**Move ahead 2**
I will _____ if…	Shake the teacher's hand.	Our teacher will be _____ if…	If I play a smartphone game later, _____.

Move ahead 2	First Conditional Structure		
	If goes first	If I catch a cold,	I will see the doctor..
	If goes second (no comma)	I will see the doctor	if I catch a cold.

If I get a high score on the English test, I will…	Stand up until your next turn.	I won't play soccer outside if…	If I get a pet, _____.
			Move back 3
If I feel bored tomorrow at school, I will…	I will… if my smartphone breaks.	Stand on one foot until your next turn!	If you _____, I will flip out. hint: look at the next page!
Move back 3			
If I eat a snack after class, I will…	If I save enough money, I will…	If I catch a cold, I will…	If it rains, I will…

1st Conditional

Let's Start!

Practice

Directions: Answer the questions about your own life. Use the first conditional.

Example

What will you do if your smartphone breaks?
<u>*If my smartphone breaks, I will bring it to the repair shop.*</u>

① If you are hungry after class, what snack will you eat?
_____

② What kind of ice cream will you eat if it is hot tomorrow?
_____

③ If your best friend is sick tomorrow, what will you do?
_____

④ If you save enough money, what will you buy?
_____

⑤ What will you do if you don't have homework tonight?
_____

⑥ If the weather is bad on Saturday, what will you do?
_____

⑦ If you go out to eat tonight, what restaurant will you visit?
_____

⑧ If the weather is cold tomorrow, what will you wear?
_____

⑨ If you catch a cold this month, what will you do?
_____

⑩ If you want to read a book later today, what book will you read?
_____

Write and answer your own first conditional question:
_____?
_____.

Everyday Language Tip

flip out = be very angry

Ex.
If our flight is delayed again, I'll **flip out!**

117

Model Conversations

Directions: Read the conversations with your partner. Pay attention to the **Reaction Responses** and **Tell-Me-More Questions**. Add these responses and questions to your notebook.

Reaction Responses	Tell-Me-More Questions
A **Reaction Response** is used to respond or react.	**Tell-Me-More Questions** ask for more information.
Not sure For real? I'm sorry to hear that. _____ _____	Do you think _____? _____ _____

A: Hi Mickey, what are you going to do tonight?
B: Not sure. You?
A: There's a big soccer game tonight! I'm going with my dad and we have an extra ticket. **Do you think** you can go with us?
B: For real? I have a math test tomorrow, **so** I should probably study. If I don't study, I will fail.
A: Well, I am really good at math, **so** I can help you study.
B: Wow, thanks a lot, Mickey.
A: No problem.

Directions: Now, fill in the blanks with the **Reaction Responses** and **Tell-Me-More Questions**.

Do you think…?   not sure   For real?   so   I'm sorry to hear that

A: A huge snowstorm is coming!

B: _____? _____ they will cancel school?

A: I'm _____. If school is canceled, what will you do?

B: If we have no school, I'll build a snowman! You?

A: I hate snow.

B: Oh, _____. Then, if it snows, what will you do?

A: I don't like the winter, _____ I'll stay inside and drink hot chocolate.

Text Me

Directions: Create new conversations with your partner. No talking!

A: What will you do _____?

B: If the weather is _____, I will _____.

A:

B:

A:

B:

A:

B:

Grade Yourself!			
Level 1	Level 2	Level 3	Level 4
Conversation Amateur	Conversation Rookie	Conversation Pro	Conversation Master
▲ Asks or answers a question	▲ Asks or answers a question ■ Uses a Reaction Response	▲ Asks or answers a question ■ Uses a Reaction Response ★ Asks a Tell-Me-More Question	▲ Asks or answers a question ■ Uses a Reaction Response ★ Asks a Tell-Me-More Question ⚡ Uses **because** or **so**

Real-Life Conversation

Directions: Have a short conversation using each question. Try to use the **Reaction Responses** and **Tell-Me-More Questions** in your conversation. Remember, all of your conversations should include **because** or **so**!

Student A

- If you are hungry after class, what snack will you eat?
- What kind of ice cream will you eat if it is hot tomorrow?
- If your husband/wife is sick tomorrow, what will you do?
- If you save enough money, what will you buy?
- What will you do if you don't have homework tonight?
- If you don't like tomorrow's cafeteria lunch, what will you do?
- If you want to exercise later today, what activity will you do?
- What will happen if you are late for school or work tomorrow morning?
- What will you do if your umbrella breaks and it rains hard?
- Who will you ask for help if you have to carry something heavy?

Conversation Checklist

- I asked a question.
- I answered a question.
- I used a **Reaction Response**.
- I asked a **Tell-Me-More** question.
- I used **because** or **so**.

Real-Life Conversation

Directions: Have a short conversation using each question. Try to use the **Reaction Responses** and **Tell-Me-More Questions** in your conversation. Remember, all of your conversations should include **because** or **so**!

Student B

- What will you do if the weather is bad on Saturday?
- If you go out to eat tonight, what restaurant will you visit?
- What will you wear if the weather is cold tomorrow?
- If you catch a cold this month, what will you do?
- If you want to read a book later today, what book will you read?
- What will you do if you feel bored at school or work tomorrow?
- If you get a pet, what animal will you choose?
- What will you do if your classmate or co-worker talks too much?
- If you listen to music after class, what song (or singer/band) will you listen to?
- How will you feel if you have three hours of homework tomorrow?

Conversation Checklist

- ○ I <u>asked</u> a question.
- ○ I <u>answered</u> a question.
- ○ I used a **Reaction Response**.
- ○ I asked a **Tell-Me-More** question.
- ○ I used **because** or **so**.

Everyday Language

Review 2

Directions: Match the Everyday Language with its meaning.

1. flip out____
2. top-notch____
3. on the same page____
4. in the blink of an eye____
5. from scratch____
6. piece of cake____
7. over the moon____
8. health nut____
9. cost an arm and a leg____
10. under the weather____
11. second to none____
12. go bananas____

A. sick
B. very happy
C. from the beginning; with basic ingredients
D. very expensive
E. excitedly celebrate
F. to show that you are very angry
G. the best
H. in agreement
I. very easy
J. very quickly
K. someone who lives a very healthy lifestyle
L. high quality

Directions: Choose the best definition.

1. couch potato
   A. a delicious snack
   B. a lazy person
   C. a fun toy

2. have a blast
   A. to have a fun and exciting time
   B. to be the best
   C. to study hard

3. twenty-four seven
   A. rarely
   B. always
   C. sometimes

4. up in the air
   A. very high
   B. not decided
   C. sad

5. hit the books
   A. to study hard
   B. to be lazy
   C. to punch a book

6. once in a blue moon
   A. sometimes
   B. rarely
   C. always

7. call it a day
   A. to finish work and go home
   B. to wake up early
   C. to call home once a day

8. down the road
   A. sometime in the future
   B. sometime in the past
   C. right now

Everyday Language conversation

see page 135

Directions: Fill in the blanks with the correct Everyday Language. Pay attention to verb tense.

hit the books	from scratch	cost an arm and a leg	in the blink of an eye	couch potato
on the same page	over the moon	once in a blue moon	second to none	go bananas
under the weather	top-notch	health nut	call it a day	piece of cake
have a blast	flip out	twenty-four seven	down the road	up in the air

1. A: Can you change the lightbulb in the bathroom?
   B: Sure, no problem. That's a _____.

2. A: What are you going to do later?
   B: I have a big test tomorrow, so I'm going to _____.

3. A: The Internet said that this is the most delicious chocolate cake in the world!
   B: Yes, I ate it last weekend. It's _____.

4. A: I am such a _____. What should I do?
   B: Get off the sofa, go outside, and exercise!

5. A: I have great news! Jose is going to go to Harvard next year!
   B: Wow! I'm _____. That is amazing!

6. A: Hey, do you want to go to dinner with us after work?
   B: Thanks for asking but I'm so tired. I'm going to _____.

7. A: How often do you visit your parents in Guatemala?
   B: _____. Almost never.

8. A: I want to join the new health club but it _____.
   B: Yes, I know. It's so expensive.

9. A: You look a little _____. Are you OK?
   B: Yes, I was sick all weekend.

10 A: I want to buy a _____ bottle of wine for my dad. What should I buy?
    B: You should go to the wine store and ask the manager.

11. A: My sister makes the most delicious guacamole _____. Do you want to try it?
    B: Yes, please!

12. A: Hey, how was your vacation? You went to South Africa, right?
    B: Yes, we got home yesterday. We _____!

13. A: You should take a break from studying for your final exams.
    B: I know! I feel like I am studying _____.

14. A: What are your plans for the future?
    B: Sometime _____, I'd like to get married and have a family. But now I'm trying to find a good job and save some money.

15. A: Did you hear about Miguel? He bought a new smartphone and then he dropped it in a puddle of water.
    B: Yes, I heard. He _____!

16. A: Hey, let's eat Vietnamese food tonight. I want to eat noodles.
    B: Me too. We're _____.

17. A: Dina is such a _____. She does yoga in the morning and goes jogging in the evening.
    B: I wish I was motivated like that.

18. A: This rollercoaster is so fast. The ride is finished _____.
    B: Really? I want to go on it too!

19. A: I am going to _____ if I win this English speech competition.
    B: Good luck! I hope you win.

20. A: What are you going to do this weekend?
    B: Our plans are _____. We might see a movie or go to the science museum.

Check your answers on page 137

Tell-Me-More Question Challenge 2

Directions: For each statement, write an appropriate **Tell-Me-More Question**. Make up your own question for 5 points.

Christmas is my favorite holiday.	Points
What do you	1
When	2
Who	3
Where	4
	5

Puppies are cuter than kittens.	Points
Do you have a	1
Do you think	2
How	3
Where	4
	5

I prefer summer to winter.	Points
Why	1
Where do you	2
How often	3
When	4
	5

My favorite ice cream flavor is strawberry.	Points
How often do you	1
What brand do	2
Who	3
Where	4
	5

You should order pepperoni and mushroom pizza.	Points
Why should I order	1
What is your	2
How often	3
Where	4
	5

Math is the most interesting subject.	Points
Why do you think	1
How often	2
Who is your	3
Where	4
	5

Reaction Response Practice 2

Directions: Read the dialogues and fill in the blanks with an appropriate **Reaction Response**. You can also use your own **Reaction Responses**. Notice all of the *Tell-Me-More Questions* in italics.

A: What's your favorite sport?

B: _____. I like soccer because I love to kick the ball. *How about you?*

A: I love basketball.

B: _____? *How often do you play?*

A: I hurt my foot last week, so I can't play until it heals.

B: _____

A: Which season do you prefer, summer or winter?

B: _____. I'm not sure. *You?*

A: I prefer summer _____ the weather is nice and I can play outside.

B: _____

A: Do you think summer is more fun than winter?

B: Actually, I love snow, _____ I love the winter. But, I also enjoy the summer too!

A: _____

B: What do you like to do in the summer?

A: I like to go swimming and eat ice cream.

B: _____

Reaction Responses
1. To show you **understand** or are **interested**: • I see. • Oh yeah? • That's cool. • Really? • Is that right? • Got it. • Is that so? • Totally!
2. To give your **opinion**: • I think...
3. To show **surprise**: • Really?!? • Seriously? • For real?
4. To say "**I don't know**": • I'm not sure. • That's a tough question. • That's a hard question. • That's an easy question.
To **agree**: ★ I agree with you. ★ I totally agree with you.
To **disagree**: ★ I disagree with you. ★ I completely disagree with you.
To show **empathy** regarding bad news: ★That's too bad. ★I'm sorry to hear that.
Others: ★ Bingo! ★ Sounds good to me.
because   so

A: Which subject is the hardest subject at school?

B: _____. I think math is

the hardest _____ there is a lot of

homework. What do you think?

A: I _____!

My math teacher never gives us homework!

B: _____.

A: Yes!

B: _____ I'm jealous of you.

A: Do you prefer salty food or sweet food?

B: Can you guess?

A: Hmmm, I think you like sweet

food more than salty food.

B: _____!

Cake is my favorite. You?

A: I don't like eating a lot of sugar, _____

I prefer salty foods.

B: What's your favorite salty food?

A: I enjoy potato chips _____ they're

salty and crunchy!

B: _____.

Reaction Responses
To show you **understand** or are **interested**: • I see • Oh yeah? • That's cool • Really? • Is that right? • Got it. • Is that so? • Totally!
To give your **opinion**: • I think...
To show **surprise**: • Really?!? • Seriously? • For real? • That's so cool!
To say "**I don't know**": • I'm not sure • That's a tough question... • That's a hard question...
To **agree**: ★ I agree with you. ★ I totally agree with you.
To **disagree**: ★ I disagree with you. ★ I completely disagree with you.
To show **empathy** regarding bad news: ★That's too bad. ★I'm sorry to hear that.
Others: ★ Bingo! ★ Sounds good to me.
because   so

Be the Teacher 2

Level 1 Conversation Amateur	Level 2 Conversation Rookie	Level 3 Conversation Pro	Level 4 Conversation Master
▲ Asks or answers a question	▲ Asks or answers a question ■ Uses a Reaction Response	▲ Asks or answers a question ■ Uses a Reaction Response ★ Asks a Tell-Me-More Question	▲ Asks or answers a question ■ Uses a Reaction Response ★ Asks a Tell-Me-More Question ⚡ Uses **because** or **so**

Directions:

If the student asks or answers a question draw ▲

If the student uses a Reaction Response draw ■

If the student uses a Tell-Me-More Questions draw ★

If the student uses because or so draw, ⚡

Example

A: I have a terrible stomachache. What should I do? ▲
B: Well, you should take some medicine. ▲
A: I took some medicine but it's not working. ▲ Should I take more medicine? ▲
B: No, you shouldn't take too much medicine. I have a good idea■. How about drinking some ginger tea ★? You should drink my tea because ginger is good for your stomach. ⚡
A: I hope so■. I'll give it a try.

	▲	■	★	⚡	Score
Student A	▲	■	★		Level 3
Student B	▲	■	★	⚡	Level 4

Directions:

If the student asks or answers a question draw ▲

If the student uses a Reaction Response draw ■

If the student uses a Tell-Me-More Questions ★

If the student uses because or so draw, ⚡

A: A huge snowstorm is coming our way.
B: Woohoo! Do you think they will cancel school?
A: Not sure. If school is canceled, what will you do?
B: If we have no school, I'll build a snowman! You?
A: For real? I hate snow, so I'll stay inside and drink hot chocolate.

	▲	■	★	⚡	Score
Student A					
Student B					

A: Do you prefer PE or lunchtime?
B: Good question. I prefer PE to lunchtime because PE is my favorite subject.
A: Can you guess which one I prefer?
B: Hmm. Lunch?
A: Bingo! I love to eat, so I prefer lunchtime to PE. What did you do in PE today?
B: We played dodgeball. It was great! What did you have for lunch?
A: I ate chicken soup, a sandwich, and a salad. It was delicious.
B: Sounds good.

	▲	■	★	⚡	Score
Student A					
Student B					

Conversation Test
Part 2

TIP: Record your conversation with a smartphone or other recording device!

Student A

Directions:

Step 1: <u>Choose 1</u> question from each unit by marking a ✓
Step 2: <u>Write 2</u> of your own questions
Step 3: Take turns asking and answering the questions (selected and written) with your partner. Remember, each conversation should **include Reaction Responses, Tell-Me-More Questions**, and **Because** and **So**. Conversations should be at least 8 lines long.
Step 4: Grade your test *(must use a recording device for this step)*.

Unit 5 Choose 1	●What's your favorite kind of weather? ●What's your favorite "Mom's cooking"? ●What's your favorite holiday? ●Who is your favorite actor or athlete? ●What's your favorite vegetable?	●What's your favorite animal? ●Who's your favorite TV star? ●What's your favorite smell? ●What's your favorite book? ●What's your favorite drink?
Unit 6 Choose 1	●Is it better to be rich and ugly or poor and beautiful/handsome? ●Which is tastier, chocolate chip cookies or brownies? ●Which is more entertaining, playing smartphone games or playing board games? ●Which is prettier, sunrise or sunset? ●Do you think water or juice is more refreshing?	●Who is a better cook, you or your husband/wife? ●Do you think reading or writing is more interesting? ●Which is more delicious, restaurant food or your Mom's home cooking? ●Which pet is cuter, a puppy or a kitten? ●Which job is more difficult, teacher or chef?
Unit 7 Choose 1	●What is the cutest animal? ●What is the spiciest food? ●What is the sourest fruit? ●What is the best city in the world? ●What is the greatest movie?	●Who is the kindest person you know? ●Who is the oldest person in your family? ●Which month is the hottest in your country? ●Who is the wisest person you know? ●Where is the best place to go on vacation?
Unit 8 Choose 1	●Do you prefer bananas or watermelon? ●Do you prefer running or riding a bike? ●Do you prefer reading or writing? ●Which do you prefer, watching the news or reading the news? ●Do you prefer hot drinks or cold drinks?	●Do you prefer giving presents or getting presents? ●Which do you prefer, standing up or sitting down? ●Do you prefer fast food or Mom's home cooking? ●Do you prefer working in a group or working alone? ●Do you prefer coffee or tea?
Unit 9 Choose 1	●What healthy foods should I eat? ●I want to have an adventurous vacation. Where should I go? ●I am visiting your hometown. Suggest a delicious restaurant for me. ●What are two things a person should do to be rich? ●Should elementary school students study a foreign language?	●What should you do when there is an earthquake? ●I am going to America next week. Where should I go? ●I have a terrible cold. What should I do? ●There is a strong storm coming this way. What should I do? ●I want to live in another country for one year. Where should I move?
Unit 10 Choose 1	●If you want to eat a snack after class, what snack will you eat? ●What kind of ice cream will you eat if it is hot tomorrow? ●If your husband/wife is sick tomorrow, what will you do? ●If you save enough money, what will you buy? ●What will you do if you don't have homework?	●If you don't like tomorrow's cafeteria lunch, what will you do? ●If you want to exercise later today, what activity will you do? ●What will happen if you are late for school or work tomorrow morning? ●What will you do if your umbrella breaks and it rains hard? ●Who will you ask for help if you have to carry something heavy?
Your Questions	Write two of your own questions. A. _____ B. _____	

Conversation Test

Part 2

> *TIP*
> Record your conversation with a smartphone or other recording device!

Student B

Directions:

Step 1: <u>Choose 1</u> question from each unit by marking a ✓
Step 2: <u>Write 2</u> of your own questions
Step 3: Take turns asking and answering the questions (selected and written) with your partner. Remember, each conversation should include **Reaction Responses, Tell-Me-More Questions**, and **Because** and **So**. Conversations should be at least 8 lines long.
Step 4: Grade your test *(must use a recording device for this step)*.

Unit 5 Choose 1	●What's your favorite food? ●What's your favorite movie? ●What's your favorite subject? ●What's your favorite fast-food restaurant? ●What's your favorite fruit?	●What's your favorite ice cream flavor? ●Who's your favorite band or singer? ●What's your favorite time of day? ●Who's your favorite teacher? ●Who's your best friend?
Unit 6 Choose 1	●Which is better for your health, a good diet or regular exercise? ●Do you think English or Spanish is harder? ●Is it better to live in a small house or a big apartment? ●Which is more enjoyable, going to a funny movie or a delicious restaurant? ●Which sport is more fun to play, soccer or badminton?	●Who is smarter, you or your brother/sister? ●Which is more fun, action movies or animated movies? ●Do you think December or January is colder? ●Which is better, getting 100% on a test or getting $50 for your birthday? ●Who is funnier, Mom or Dad?
Unit 7 Choose 1	●What's your mom's most delicious recipe? ●What's the most popular place to visit in your country? ●What is the best show on TV? ●What is the most interesting subject to study? ●What is the most exciting game?	●Who is the most creative person you know? ●What is the coolest car? ●What is the most disgusting food? ●What is the most boring subject in school? ●Which month is the coldest in your country?
Unit 8 Choose 1	●Do you prefer spaghetti or steak? ●Do prefer monkeys or rabbits? ●Which do you prefer, soccer or basketball? ●Do you prefer action movies or comedy movies? ●Do you prefer spring or fall?	●Do you prefer dogs or cats? ●Do you prefer computer games or smartphone games? ●Do you prefer taking the bus or taking the train? ●Which do you prefer, eating at home or eating at a restaurant? ●Do you like cold weather or hot weather?
Unit 9 Choose 1	●Should children have smartphones? ●What movie should I watch next weekend? ●Suggest a great book for me to read. ●What pizza toppings should I order? ●How often should I exercise?	●What should you do when there is a fire? ●What are two things a person should do to be healthy? ●I lost my smartphone. What should I do? ●I found a twenty-dollar bill on the street. What should I do? ●My friend hates spicy food. What foreign food should we eat?
Unit 10 Choose 1	●What will you do if the weather is bad on Saturday? ●If you go out to eat tonight, what restaurant will you visit? ●What will you wear if the weather is cold tomorrow? ●If you catch a cold this month, what will you do? ●If you want to read a book later today, what book will you read?	●What will you do if you feel bored at school or work tomorrow? ●If you get a pet, what animal will you choose? ●What will you do if your classmate or co-worker talks too much? ●If you listen to music after class, what song (or singer/band) will you listen to? ●How will you feel if you have three hours of homework tomorrow?
Your Questions	Write two of your own questions. 1. _____ 2. _____	

Grade Your Test

Directions:

★ Choose two of your conversation questions.
★ Listen and transcribe your conversations.
★ Use the rubric to grade yourself.

Conversation 1
A: _____
B: _____
A: _____
B: _____
A: _____
B: _____
A: _____
B: _____
A: _____
B: _____

If the student asks or answers a question draw ▲

If the student uses a Reaction Response draw ■

If the student uses a Tell-Me-More Questions draw ★

If the student uses **because** or **so** draw, ⚡

	▲	■	★	⚡	Score
Student A					
Student B					

Conversation 2

A: _____

B: _____

A: _____

B: _____

A: _____

B: _____

A: _____

B: _____

A: _____

B: _____

If the student asks or answers a question draw ▲

If the student uses a Reaction Response draw ■

If the student uses a Tell-Me-More Questions draw ★

If the student uses because or so draw, ⚡

	▲	■	★	⚡	Score
Student A					
Student B					

Everyday Language Conversation

Directions: Have a short conversation with each question. Try to use **Reaction Responses**, **Tell-Me-More Questions**, and **because** or **so** in your conversation.

Student A
1. Do you know any **couch potatoes**?
2. Which restaurant is **second to none**?
3. When do you usually **call it a day**?
4. What recipe does your mom make **from scratch**?
5. Do you stay home from work or school when you are **under the weather**?
6. What exercise is a **piece of cake** for you?
7. What is something you think about **twenty-four seven**?
8. Should elementary school students spend more time having fun or **hitting the books**?
9. Are you **on the same page** as your best friend or do you disagree often?
10. When is the last time you were **over the moon**?

Student B
1. What is something you want to buy that **costs an arm and a leg**?
2. Do you know any **health nuts**?
3. What food do you eat **once in a blue moon**?
4. When is the last time **you had a blast**?
5. How often do you **go bananas**?
6. What decision is **up in the air**?
7. What is a **top-notch** product from your country?
8. When is the last time your friend **flipped out**?
9. What experience is over **in the blink of an eye**?
10. What are your plans **down the road**?

Rubrics

Level 1 Conversation Amateur	Level 2 Conversation Rookie	Level 3 Conversation Pro
▲ Asks or answers a question	▲ Asks or answers a question ■ Uses a Reaction Response	▲ Asks or answers a question ■ Uses a Reaction Response ★ Asks a Tell-Me-More Question

Conversation Checklist

O I <u>asked</u> a question.

O I <u>answered</u> a question.

O I used a **Reaction Response**.

O I asked a **Tell-Me-More Question**.

Conversation Checklist

O I <u>asked</u> a question.

O I <u>answered</u> a question.

O I used a **Reaction Response**.

O I asked a **Tell-Me-More Question**.

O I used **because** or **so**.

Level 1 Conversation Amateur	Level 2 Conversation Rookie	Level 3 Conversation Pro	Level 4 Conversation Master
▲ Asks or answers a question	▲ Asks or answers a question ■ Uses a Reaction Response	▲ Asks or answers a question ■ Uses a Reaction Response ★ Asks a Tell-Me-More Question	▲ Asks or answers a question ■ Uses a Reaction Response ★ Asks a Tell-Me-More Question ⚡ Uses **because** or **so**

Everyday Language Review Answers

pg. 49

Part 1
1. H
2. A
3. G
4. F
5. B
6. E
7. C
8. D

Part 2
1. couch potato
2. had a blast
3. hit the books
4. once in a blue moon
5. twenty-four seven
6. called it a day
7. up in the air
8. down the road

Everyday Language Review 2 Answers

pg. 122

Part 1
1. F
2. L
3. H
4. J
5. C
6. I
7. B
8. K
9. D
10. A
11. G
12. E

Part 2
1. B
2. A
3. B
4. B
5. A
6. B
7. A

8. A

Part 3
1. piece of cake
2. hit the books
3. second to none
4. couch potato
5. over the moon
6. call it a day
7. once in a blue moon
8. costs an arm and a leg
9. under the weather
10. top-notch
11. from scratch
12. had a blast
13. twenty-four seven
14. down the road
15. flipped out
16. on the same page
17. health nut
18. in the blink of an eye
19. go bananas
20. up in the air

About the Author

Brian Branca has been living and teaching EFL in South Korea for the last seven years. During his time in Korea, he has taught EFL classes at every level. Brian is currently an English instructor at Youngsan University in Yangsan, South Korea.

Before Korea, Brian received his teacher training at the Academy of Urban School Leadership (AUSL) in Chicago, IL. While training to be a high school English teacher, Brian earned a Master's in the Art of Teaching from National Louis University (MAT '07). He then went on to teach English and language arts at Al Raby High School in the Chicago Public Schools. During his time at Al Raby, Brian earned a second master's degree in curriculum from DePaul University (MA '10).

Brian and his brother, Daniel, recently created an ESL/EFL website called myenglisheets.com. The mission of the website is to equip busy ESL/EFL teachers with free, high-quality, instructional materials and to provide students with relevant and authentic opportunities to speak English.

Also by ESL Publishing

US Citizenship Bootcamp by Jennifer Gagliardi

When students prepare for their Citizenship interview, they usually focus on memorizing the 100 Civics and History questions. However, when they go to the interview, they are often surprised that the USCIS (United States Citizenship and Immigration Services) examiner asks 20 to 70 questions from the N-400 Application for Naturalization, and only six to 10 Civics questions, PLUS the students must read and write one sentence in English.

This book is an attempt to help students prepare for their Citizenship interview by presenting 10 interviews based on the N-400, in order of increasing vocabulary and grammatical difficulty.

Highlights:
- An overview of the Naturalization Process
- Practice N-400 Questions based on the new USCIS N-400
- Practice Civics Questions based on the new USCIS N-400
- Practice Quizzes and Answers
- Vocabulary words and definitions
- Helpful tips for comprehending and answering interview questions
- Helpful hints for the US Citizenship interview
- Easy-to-read charts to help with comprehension and learning
- Internet citizenship resources and links

This book can be ordered online with a discount for bulk orders.

www.eslpublishing.com

She Built Ships During World War II is a historical novel for English language learners at the intermediate level. It is an excellent way for a student to learn history and English at the same time. The novel can stand alone or be used in conjunction with the companion workbook (published separately), which is designed for use along with the novel in language classes. The workbook has a rich variety of vocabulary, word-building, and comprehension exercises, as well as writing, discussion, and critical-thinking topics for use in the language classroom. Original novel by Jeane Slone. ESL revision by Michelle Deya Knoop.

With meticulous research on the WWII era, Slone weaves an intricate story of cruelty, compassion, and love, reminding us of the injustice of the internment of Japanese Americans and racial prejudice in the armed forces. The courage of women welders who built ships while their husbands were at war is depicted so well that the characters come to life. We watch the heroine, Lolly, struggle to keep her family together while she works as a welder and her husband is away. A tender romance is threaded throughout the book, and we agonize with her as she brings it to an inevitable conclusion. Between the fascinating and sometimes little-known historical facts, and the larger-than-life sympathetic characters, the book is a page-turner to the very end.

— Alla Crone, author of *Winds Over Manchuria*, *East Lies the Sun*, and *Russian Bride*

This workbook is designed to be used in combination with the novel, *She Built Ships During World War II*, in language classes or self-study. Intended to build vocabulary at the intermediate level, it has a variety of words, phrases, and idioms, word-building, structure, and reading comprehension exercises. In addition, it includes writing, discussion, and critical-thinking topics designed for use in the language or reading classroom. Workbook by Michelle Deya Knoop.

Highlights:
- Vocabulary and idioms are presented and practiced in the context of the novel's storyline.
- Word form and structure exercises support and develop the new vocabulary.
- Critical thinking, writing, and pair/group discussion topics inspire readers to explore the social, personal, ethical, and moral issues raised in the novel.

These books can be ordered online with a discount for bulk orders.

www.eslpublishing.com